Thomas Twining

Travels in America 100 years ago. Being notes and reminiscences

Thomas Twining

Travels in America 100 years ago. Being notes and reminiscences

ISBN/EAN: 9783337207908

Printed in Europe, USA, Canada, Australia, Japan

Cover: Foto ©Andreas Hilbeck / pixelio.de

More available books at **www.hansebooks.com**

THOMAS TWINING

TRAVELS IN AMERICA
100 YEARS AGO

BEING NOTES AND REMINISCENCES

By THOMAS TWINING

NEW YORK
HARPER & BROTHERS PUBLISHERS
1894

Harper's "Black and White" Series.

Illustrated. 32mo, Cloth, 50 cents each.

- TRAVELS IN AMERICA 100 YEARS AGO. By Thomas Twining.
- MY YEAR IN A LOG CABIN. By William Dean Howells.
- EVENING DRESS. A Farce. By William Dean Howells.
- THE WORK OF WASHINGTON IRVING. By Charles Dudley Warner.
- EDWIN BOOTH. By Laurence Hutton.
- THE DECISION OF THE COURT. A Comedy. By Brander Matthews.
- PHILLIPS BROOKS. By Rev. Arthur Brooks, D.D.
- GEORGE WILLIAM CURTIS. By John White Chadwick.
- THE UNEXPECTED GUESTS. A Farce. By William Dean Howells.
- SLAVERY AND THE SLAVE TRADE IN AFRICA. By Henry M. Stanley.
- THE RIVALS. By François Coppée.
- WHITTIER: NOTES OF HIS LIFE AND OF HIS FRIENDSHIPS. By Annie Fields.
- THE JAPANESE BRIDE. By Naomi Tamura.
- GILES COREY, YEOMAN. By Mary E. Wilkins.
- COFFEE AND REPARTEE. By John Kendrick Bangs.
- JAMES RUSSELL LOWELL. An Address. By George William Curtis.
- SEEN FROM THE SADDLE. By Isa Carrington Cabell.
- A FAMILY CANOE TRIP. By Florence Watters Snedeker.
- A LITTLE SWISS SOJOURN. By William Dean Howells.
- A LETTER OF INTRODUCTION. A Farce. By William Dean Howells.
- IN THE VESTIBULE LIMITED. By Brander Matthews.
- THE ALBANY DEPOT. A Farce. By William Dean Howells.

PUBLISHED BY HARPER & BROTHERS, NEW YORK

For sale by all booksellers, or will be sent by the publishers, postage prepaid, on receipt of price.

Copyright, 1893, by HARPER & BROTHERS.

All rights reserved.

INTRODUCTION

THOMAS TWINING was one of the energetic Englishmen who laid the foundations of the Indian Empire. He arrived in India, as he told his English neighbors in a lecture delivered forty-six years afterwards, a puny boy of sixteen, in 1792. He quitted it finally in 1805, still under thirty. In the interval, to quote his own words, he "had been intrusted with the reform of an extensive department of the public administration, had been appointed judge of a great district, had held the charge of a country containing more than ten thousand towns and villages, and more than two millions of people, and had been received by the Great Mogul on his throne in the old world and by General Washington in the new."

His visit to the United States, almost at the beginning of our national existence, was an episode in his Indian career, occurring in the course of his return to England between two terms of residence in India. It seems to have been solely a visit of curiosity, and readers of the account of it now presented to the American public will agree that they are much indebted to his curiosity, and to the record that he left of its assuagement. Authentic statements of the impression made upon intelligent and unprejudiced foreigners by the narrow strip of seaboard that virtually constituted the territory of the young republic are not so common that an addition to the short list will not be welcome.

After his return to England Mr. Twining married, and for a time settled in Northamptonshire, but after Waterloo lived with his family for twenty years upon the Continent. Returning to England in 1837, he settled at Twickenham, and died there in 1861.

AMERICA

1795.—The state of my health rendering a voyage to Europe necessary, I determined to proceed by way of America. Accordingly, towards the end of November, I left Santipore, taking with me a small Bengal cow, in addition to my doombah and other curiosities brought from Dehli. The natives would not have consented to sell me a cow if I had not assured them that it would be an object of particular interest and care in the countries I was taking it to. I also had made, by an ingenious workman of Santipore, small, but very exact, models of the principal machines and instruments used in the agriculture and manufactures of India. Among these was a model of an Indian plough, and an excellent one of an Indian loom, with the threads upon it, executed with remarkable precision and neatness. With all these objects I arrived, by the Ganges, at my old quarters in Captain Thornhill's house.

One of my first visits was to the commander of the American ship *India*, Captain John Ashmead. He was a Quaker; a tall, thin, upright man of about sixty or perhaps sixty-five, in whose respectable and pleasing appearance the usual mildness and simplicity of his sect, with a deep tinge of characteristic peculiarity, were visible. His thin silvery locks curled round the collar of his old-fashioned single-breasted coat, with a row of large plain buttons down the front like a schoolboy's. He introduced me to the supercargo, a Scotchman. The same evening the captain accompanied me to the ship. This I found rather smaller than I had expected. Her measurement was only about 300 tons. But everything on board was seamanlike and neat. The upper deck was flush — that is, level — from head to stern, without any cabin upon it, as in the *Ponsborne*. The lower deck, to which the descent was by a straight ladder from the quarter-deck, had a spacious cabin or dining-room towards the stern, comprehending the whole width of the ship and lighted by the stern windows. I agreed for the starboard half of this room, consenting to its being separated from the other half by a green baize curtain, which was to be drawn back along a brass rod at the hours of dinner and breakfast. The dining-table was fixed in the middle of the room, and half of it consequently remained in my cabin when the curtain was drawn.

As the ship was to sail in a few days, I had not much time to prepare for my voyage. The American captains having the reputation of keeping rather an indifferent table—living, it was said, principally on salt beef and sour-crout—Mr. Fletcher had the goodness to send me ten fat sheep from his flock at Santipore. For these and my cow and doombah, a considerable quantity of hay was necessary. I therefore ordered my servants to buy grass, or rather the *roots* of grass, in the bazaars, and which, being spread and exposed to the sun upon the flat roofs of Captain Thornhill's outhouses, was closely pressed into bundles.

To increase my collection of objects relating to India, I bought, at a sale by auction, some oil-paintings executed by an able European artist. One represented an elephant with a howdah upon his back, kneeling to be mounted; another exhibited two or three zuz, a small leopard of elegant form, used in hunting the antelope. They were muzzled and had collars round their necks, and were led by their attendants like greyhounds to the chase. But the most valuable addition was that which my menagerie received, consisting of a Thibet or shawl goat, presented to me by my friend, Mr. Myers, Deputy Accountant-General. This animal was a curiosity even in Calcutta. It was small, thin, and scraggy, and had long hair, principally black, with some white about the neck and legs. Upon dividing this long hair a short white soft wool was seen, covering the body like down, and this was the precious material from which the shawl of Cashmire is fabricated. It being much doubted and disputed whether it was a *goat* or a *sheep* which produced this substance, I considered myself fortunate in being able to exhibit in America and Europe such decisive testimony upon this point. I had, however, some uneasiness from the apparently delicate state of the goat's health, which seemed to have suffered from the damp climate of Calcutta.

In the first days of December, the *India*, having completed her lading, dropped down the river, and in two days more I followed her. I left the ghaut of the Bankshall (the name of Captain Thornhill's office) late in the evening in a pauchway, a small covered boat rowed by four men seated before the roofed part, and steered by a fifth, who stood behind it. The good captain and his son, Mr. John Thornhill, accompanied me to the water's edge. The tide running very rapidly, I was far advanced at daybreak next morning, and in the afternoon reached the ship, which was anchored not far from the point where I had disembarked from the *Ponsborne* in 1792. I spent the remainder of the day in arranging my things in my cabin, in fixing my excellent English trunks, which I had fortunately preserved, and in securing a teakwood bedstead, with drawers under it, which I had bought in the bazaar of Calcutta. The upper part, with the bedding upon it, was made to be lifted up from the drawers, and to serve as a swinging cot in rough weather. The small white cow, Cabul sheep, Cashmire goat, and the sheep from Santipore were disposed of: some in, some under, the boats between the main and fore mast. The monkey from the North of India had a welcome reception on the forecastle among the crew.

On the 9th of December, the pilot being on board and the wind quite fair, the anchor was heaved and we set sail. Leaving Sangor Island close on our left, we passed between this and the numerous shoals and sandbanks across which the *Ponsborne* had had so narrow an escape. We saw many immense buoys of different colors moored with strong chains — some on the sands, others in the fairway or channel—to be followed by ships. But, notwithstanding these precautions and an extensive establishment of pilots under the direction of Captain Thornhill, many vessels are annually lost in this dangerous navigation. Arrived off the sand-heads, we saw a pilot schooner cruising for inward-bound ships. Having made a signal to her she approached us and received our pilot on board, when the venerable Quaker, who till now had been a quiet spectator on board his own ship, took the command. And here I could not but observe a singular contrast between this old man and my first captain— between the cool, unassuming demeanor of Captain Ashmead and the loud, authoritative manner of Captain Thomas. A difference, no less striking, was observable between the well-manned decks and simultaneous movements of the Indiaman, and the scanty crew and slow, consecutive operations of the American ship. For, the whole crew of the latter being only twenty-two men, the principal work of the three masts, instead of going on at the same time, as in the *Ponsborne*, was necessarily done in succession; the men descending from one mast to mount another, hoisting the foretop-sail first and the maintop-sail afterwards. I observed, also, that of our numbers thus small, the greater part consisted of very young men, apparently not more than eighteen or twenty years of age. They were better dressed than the sailors I had been accustomed to see, and had altogether a more respectable, though a less robust and seaman-like appearance. The cause of this difference was, for the present, unknown to me. At first I was rather startled at this apparent inefficiency, and at the idea of undertaking the passage of the Cape of Good Hope in so small a ship so feebly manned. On the other hand, I was much pleased with the mild, inoffensive tone in which the captain gave his orders, and with the cheerful alacrity with which they were executed. There was no oath, nor threat, nor vulgar language; no anxious exertion or fearful obedience. There was nothing to damp the satisfaction and gladness of that joyful moment of a seaman's life, when, after a long voyage, the ship's head is again turned towards his native country.

We stood out of Balasore roads towards the middle of the bay, and having gained a good offing, beyond the variable breezes of the coast, steered to the south. The northwest monsoon now prevailing, and blowing fresh on our starboard quarter, we kept a straight course down the bay at about seven knots an hour. The weather was so mild and fine that for several nights I slept upon the after-part of the upper deck, over my cabin, stretched upon a hen-coop, and I found that I thus avoided all material inconvenience from sea-sickness. After five or six days I was able to take my place at the dinner-table. The party here consisted of Captain Ashmead, Mr. Pringle, the supercargo, Mr. Gilmore, Mr. Brisbane, the surgeon, a young man, who was chief mate, and myself. Mr. Gilmore was son of one of the owners of the ship, and had come to India in her with the view of learning the business of an India voyage under Mr. Pringle.

We had a fair wind and fine weather from

the sand-heads to the latitudes bordering on the line. We here experienced some light, baffling breezes, but our progress was not interrupted by those total calms so usual near the equator. The ship's head was now turned towards the Cape of Good Hope. We spent our Christmas Day not very far from the Isle of France, or Mauritius (Maurice), as it was called by the Dutch, the original possessors. On this occasion the usual salutations of the day were exchanged among us; we had a more ample dinner, and there was an extra distribution to the men, who were dressed as on Sundays. There was something impressive in the observance of this great day by our little society in the midst of the ocean. We approached nearer to the French Islands than would have been prudent for a vessel not under neutral colors, for they were the general rendezvous of the numerous privateers which had done so much injury to the British commerce in the Indian seas.

The Isle of France is situated in 20° of south latitude, the Isle of Bourbon about one hundred and fifty miles more to the south. The former is about fifty leagues in circumference, the latter about eighteen leagues in length and thirteen in width. The climate of both is said to be delightful, and to be congenial to most of the productions of the tropical regions, such as sugar, coffee, tobacco, indigo, cotton, the breadfruit-tree, etc. The population of the Isle of France is about 70,000, principally slaves procured from Madagascar. I could not help wishing that we might put into Port Louis, the chief port of this island; but neither a deficiency in our water, nor any other circumstance, requiring this deviation, our prudent captain continued his course towards the Cape, passing not far from the south end of the Island of Madagascar. In a few days more we approached the Cape of Good Hope, and the usual preparations for stormy weather were made accordingly. The captain ordering a reef in the main-sail, all hands that could be spared from deck, amounting to eighteen, went upon the main-yard. On board a man-of-war, or even an Indiaman, this operation would have required only a few minutes; but our crew, as I have already observed, was very young, and individually very weak, consisting rather of boys than men, and it consequently took a long time to haul up the sail and make it fast. The old man, however, never lost his temper or patience, and the sailors, having accomplished their task, in the quiet, orderly way in which everything was conducted on board, were descending to the deck, when one of the last of them observed that the slings which suspended the main-yard were broken; two-thirds of the twists had given way, leaving the whole weight upon one-third alone. This discovery greatly affected the captain, and caused a considerable impression through the ship, for it was evident that eighteen men who had just left the yard had been exposed to great danger. Had the yard fallen with them, all, it was probable, would have been killed or disabled. After the first impressions had subsided it became a question among us what we should have done if the threatened accident had taken place. Here our helplessness became more evident, and rendered us more sensible of our providential escape.

Continuing our course towards the west, in a few days more we got soundings, and thought we discovered land upon the starboard beam. We were upon a deep bank called Agulas's Bank, which extends more than one hundred miles to the south of the Cape. The nature of the bottom being different in different parts, it was desirable to obtain some portion of it in order to ascertain our position with more precision. For this purpose a lead was used of about a foot long and two inches in diameter, with a small cavity at the bottom filled with putty. When the lead was drawn in, sand and broken shells were found attached to it. Comparing this result with a map of the bank, our position appeared, and, confirming the ship's reckoning, the captain had no desire to see the land more distinctly. We passed first Sebastian's Bay; afterwards False Bay, which opens towards the south; and lastly Table Bay, a little round the point on the Atlantic side, and near Cape Town. The winds were now strong against us from the west, but we got on against them by aid of a strong current which always runs down the eastern coast of Africa, and sets round the land. It is for this reason that homeward-bound ships, or rather, ships bound to the west of the Cape, keep near it, *hugging the land*, as the sailors say; while those bound eastward keep to the south. Although we thus passed the Cape without encountering any particular storm, we were very near meeting with a serious accident ·of another kind. One dark night, about ten o'clock, when the wind was fresh, a seaman of the forecastle watch came running aft, exclaiming, with much agitation, "A ship ahead!" We had scarcely heard these words before a large ship, running before the wind, passed our starboard bow. As she went swiftly by us, our yard-arms almost touching, the captain had just time to hail her, and to hear in reply, as we thought, the words "Superb" and "Amsterdam," from which we inferred that she was from Holland, and bound for Batavia. Here again we had reason to be thankful, for a few feet nearer, half a turn of the wheel of either ship, and both vessels must have gone to the bottom. The agitation of the sailor, and the difficulty he had in expressing himself, reminded me of a story which Captain Thomas once told at the cuddy table, relating to a ship under his command at the time, either as commander or chief officer of the watch, and which afforded another instance of the never-failing presence of mind of that excellent seaman. One of the sailors came suddenly upon deck from below, but such was his terror that he was unable to articulate a word. "Sing!" said the captain, "sing!" when the poor man sang out without any difficulty, "The cabin's on fire! The cabin's on fire!" Captain Thomas, in his repetition, giving the man's song with excellent effect.

Passing the Cape so near the land we saw but few of the great albatrosses and other birds which had appeared on my way to India, these flying more to the south, for the sake, it was supposed, of the small fish or other food thrown up on the surface of the sea, in the storms which prevail there. Our course was now northwest, with variable winds, but principally from the south.

The first great division of the voyage being passed, the usual speculations took place as to the probable duration of the remainder. If not detained by calms at the line it was probable we should reach America in less than two months. About a fortnight after clearing the Cape the increasing unsteadiness of the wind denoted that we were upon the edge of the "Trade," and in a few days more a fresh, steady breeze from the southeast assured us of our having gained that much-desired wind.

Our course was now in the direction of St. Helena. The ship remained under nearly the same sail for many days and nights together, going at the rate of seven or eight knots an hour, rolling from one side to the other, the wind being directly astern. This is called " rolling down to St. Helena " by the captains of Indiamen. On the 10th February, lat. 25 S., long. 5 E., we discovered, in the afternoon, a sail on our starboard beam. Though a great way off, as we were evidently steering the same way, there seemed a chance of our speaking, and it being supposed that she was bound to Europe, and probably to England, I began a letter to my father. The night, however, closed upon us without our approaching. The next morning the sail was still in sight, and nearly at the same distance from us. We therefore bore up a point, and soon perceived that she accepted our invitation to speak, by making a similar variation in her course towards us. In the afternoon we were within hail, when we found that the stranger was the American ship *Atlantic*, from China, and bound, like ourselves, to Philadelphia. We kept company during the night, but separated next day. As we had the advantage in sailing, we expected to reach America some days before her.

After repassing the tropic of Capricorn, we continued our rolling course towards the northwest, and in ten days more passed the island of St. Helena, about, as we supposed, one hundred miles to the west of it. The climate was now very agreeable. The southeast trade, which still blew fresh, tempered the heat of the sun, and kept the atmosphere at a pleasant temperature.

I now passed much of my time upon deck, reading, or walking, or playing at backgammon with the captain, who was extremely fond of this game, and played it very well. In accordance with the serenity of the climate, and the evenness of our course at this part of the voyage, was the orderly and cheerful character of the ship, everything between the captain and officers and crew being conducted in the most good-tempered and amicable manner. The latter enjoyed a degree of comfort which I had never seen on board a ship. Most of the men had a few private stores, and many of them took their tea in little parties about the forecastle. I was not surprised at these indulgences, for I had learned, soon after sailing, that the young men whose genteel appearance I had noticed were the sons of respectable families of Philadelphia and Baltimore, who had come to sea under Captain Ashmead for the purpose of being instructed in navigation by this experienced seaman, preparatory to their being officers and captains themselves. While this system of harmony and decency was extremely agreeable, I could not perceive that it was less efficient, as regarded the duties of the ship, than the usual vulgar system of oppressive severity called *discipline*. I had now been three months on board the *India*, and had not heard a threat used nor an oath uttered.

As we approached the equator I again saw, with pleasure, the swift dolphin, the flying-fish, the gelatinous substance called a Portuguese man-of-war, and the elegant tropic bird. We one day enjoyed a more unusual sight, a party of large whales making their appearance at a short distance from the ship. They rolled about on the surface of the sea, amusing themselves, apparently, as well as us. I had once considered the spouting of whales as a fabulous exaggeration, but I distinctly saw and heard these fish spout up the sea to the height of several feet, with a considerable noise or blowing. As they tumbled about for some time, not far from our larboard bow, the captain was uneasy lest we should strike against them.

But after keeping at the same distance from us for about an hour, they plunged and disappeared.

The trade wind, which had favored us some weeks, gradually declined as we drew near the equator. It did not, however, subside entirely, but took us a few degrees into the northern hemisphere, when the winds again became variable. We continued our north-western course through the northern tropic, leaving on our left the West India Islands and the Gulf of Mexico. We again saw a sail, a two-masted vessel. She was rather ahead, but lay-to for us to come up, when we perceived that her boat was out, rowing towards us. Our captain lay-to for it to reach us, but observed that the brig might be a pirate, and that it would be prudent to be on our guard while her boat was alongside and her people on board. Looking at the boat through his telescope, he said he saw only five hands, but that there might be more concealed under a tarpaulin at the bottom. Upon this he went down to his cabin, at the bottom of the ladder, and returned upon deck with a brace of pistols, which he put into his coat pockets. For the old man was not a *Quaker* in any sense but one, and was resolved to be ready to repulse any hostile attack. I did not put my pistols into my pockets, for these were far from being so deep as those of the captain; but they were ready, and in case of necessity the father of the ship, as he was considered, would certainly have been well supported by every one of his family. When, however, the boat come alongside, it was obvious that it contained no more than the persons before visible. The steersman was therefore permitted to come on board. He was the captain himself of the brig, which we now found was from Boston, but last from the Canary Islands, and bound to one of the southern parts of the United States. The captain said he had had very stormy weather in crossing the Atlantic. When, at his request, we gave him our longitude, he was much surprised, as we were when he communicated his, for there was a difference of many degrees between us. This extraordinary error was doubtless on his side, for Captain Ashmead was an excellent mathematician, possessed much nautical knowledge, and kept the ship's reckoning with great accuracy. Although, therefore, we had not had any point of departure since our soundings off the Cape, and the captain of the brig had been much less time at sea, the mistake was ascribable to the dark weather he had experienced, and in some degree, it was probable, to the imperfection of his science or of his instruments. He was fully satisfied of his having greatly misconceived the situation of his ship, and allowed it was a fortunate circumstance that he had fallen in with us. Finding that we came from Bengal, he requested a few bags of rice, which were readily given him. In return we applied to him for one or two articles, and I expressed a wish to buy a bag of sago, for my breakfast, and a few figs. As the boat was to return to our ship with these things, I went in her to the other vessel. The most remarkable circumstance I found on board was an extraordinary number of canary birds. The cabin was crowded with cages containing them. I afterwards understood that a considerable profit was obtained on the sale of these birds in the southern parts of the Union. I again recollected my mother's fancy, and should have procured a few of them, but for the probability of their perishing from want of proper care. I returned to the *India* with a small supply of sago and figs, when the vessels separated, and we continued our course towards the coast of America.

The only interesting occurrence in the remainder of our voyage was our crossing the Gulf Stream. I was surprised at seeing one day large quantities of sea-weed round the ship, and the water changed from its usual appearance to a yellow color. The waves also had a different form, exhibiting a peculiarity something like the rippling of a current. These signs denoted our arrival in the great current called by navigators the "Gulf Stream," from its proceeding from the Gulf of Mexico. The common opinion is that this current is occasioned by the constant flow of the Mississippi River into the Mexican Gulf. This explanation, however, appears by no means satisfactory, since the volume of the stream, sixteen leagues in width, greatly exceeds that of the Mississippi. Another hypothesis considers it as the continuation of the current which sets round the Cape of Good Hope from the Indian seas, and, traversing the Atlantic Ocean, nearly in the line followed by our ship, enters the Gulf of Mexico, whence it re-enters the ocean *with* the waters of the Mississippi, and follows the American coast till finally dissipated in the Northern seas. As we advanced towards the middle of the stream the quantity of weed was prodigious, covering the surface of the water as far as we could see. This phenomenon was not interesting alone, but was useful, as verifying our position in respect to the American coast.

We soon had a great change of climate, the weather becoming more cold than I had felt it since leaving England. I could hardly keep myself warm day or night. But this inconvenience was welcome as another sign that the end of our voyage was nigh. On the 1st of April the lead was heaved, but no bottom found. The captain, however, ordered the ship to be kept under easy sail during the night, her head alternately to the north and south. The lead also was frequently heaved. These precautions were not premature, for the next morning, Saturday, the 2d April, the leadsman proclaimed bottom. We lay-to that night, but the following day we again stood towards land, and I had the gratification of seeing the light-house at the entrance of Delaware Bay, after a prosperous voyage of less than four months from the mouth of the Ganges. Unfortunately no pilot appeared, although our signal for one was kept flying. Our disappointment was the greater as the weather had a threatening appearance. Some dangerous shoals, called the Nantucket Shoals, seemed to give the captain some uneasiness and to increase his desire to get into port. He said that he had been more than sixty voyages from the Delaware, and was as capable as a pilot to take the ship into the bay, but that in case of accident, from whatever cause, the insurances would be void. In the evening, therefore, no pilot appearing, the ship's head was put off shore and we stood out to sea. Mortifying as this course was, its prudence was soon manifest, for in the night the threatening aspect of the weather ended in a gale of wind. We saw nothing around us next day, but kept the lead going lest the current should set us towards the land. In the afternoon the gale increased, and there was much bustle on board. The scantiness of the crew made it necessary for every one to lend a hand on such an occasion. In consequence of an order given by the captain to let go some rope near the stern, I ran aft and did what was necessary. At this moment the rope which held the great spanker-boom to windward gave way, and this spar, with the sail upon it, immediately fell down to leeward with prodigious force. The captain said that when he saw me between the falling boom and the ship's side he thought my destruction inevitable. When, however, the boom had arrived within three or four feet of the side against which I was leaning, it was stopped by a thick block projecting from the stern rail. I never perhaps had a more providential escape.

A heavy fall of rain the second night having abated the violence of the wind, the next morning—Tuesday, the 5th April—at daybreak, we were again able to set sail on the ship and stand towards the coast. We were this time more fortunate. A sail was perceived, and the captain soon pronounced her to be a pilot making towards us. When sufficiently near he came on board in a small skiff belonging to his diminutive vessel. For this was not a schooner, as in the Bengal River, but merely a stout-decked boat, resembling a large fishing-boat. The pilot having taken charge of us, we proceeded directly towards the mouth of the Delaware River. In the afternoon we again saw the lighthouse, and, passing it early in the evening, entered Delaware Bay, having on our left

Cape Henlopen, on which the light-house stood, and on our right Cape May. The distance between the two capes was said to be fifteen miles, though appearing much less. Within them the bay gradually widened to about twenty-four miles. We passed near many shoals, particularly " Big Shoal," on which the depth of water varied from six to ten feet. On our right we had the State of New Jersey, on our left that of Delaware. Both shores appeared low and flat, but on arriving in the New World I felt an interest in everything I beheld that supplied the want of picturesque attractions. I spent the whole day upon deck asking questions and looking about me. A little before dark we came to anchor near a large buoy, called the Buoy of the Brown.

6th April.—I was early on deck, expecting the ship to get under way to mount the river, but the pilot said the tide would not be favorable for some hours. While we were at anchor several vessels and fishing-boats from Philadelphia passed us on their way to sea. We weighed soon after twelve o'clock. For some time we were near a vessel from England, also bound to Philadelphia. The captains hailed each other, and afterwards exchanged newspapers by throwing a line, having a small piece of lead at the end, on board the other ship, and then drawing it backward and forward with the papers attached to it. We steered generally in six or eight fathoms, and nearly in the middle of the bay, which gradually contracted into the Delaware River, so called after the Earl of Delaware, who settled in this part of the American continent early in the seventeenth century. A river of such magnitude and importance, and which bore the metropolis of a great nation upon its banks, seemed to claim a more dignified name than the title of an adventurous nobleman. In this respect India had been more fortunate. *There*, the British conquerors and settlers, not having had the pretension and bad taste to change the ancient names of the country for their own, Plassey was not called "Clive," nor Buxar "Munro," while the Ganges, the Burrampooter, and the Saone retained, with no material corruption, the sacred orthography of the remotest ages.

We continued to mount the river, passing between Brown's and Brandywine Shoal. On our left we passed the town of Dover, one of the principal towns of the Delaware

State. Though capes May and Henlopen, on the shore of the Atlantic, seemed to mark the commencement of the Delaware—the space called the *bay* being merely an expanded reach of the river itself—this nevertheless was not considered as beginning till we had passed Bombay Hook, twenty miles *above* the capes. Here the width was about three miles. On the Jersey side we passed Stony Point and the small town of Salem. Twenty miles above Bombay Point we came to Reedy Island, and anchored for the night at Port Penn. This seemed to be the Gravesend of the Delaware, being the usual rendezvous of ships before entering the Atlantic. The direction of our course to-day had been about north-west.

7th April.—It was late again to-day before the tide would allow us to move. Our course to-day was extremely pleasant, the river becoming more picturesque as it became more contracted. We passed several small islands; the principal of which was Delaware Island, and the considerable town of Newcastle, on the western shore, formerly called Stockholm, having been founded by the Swedes, and later New Amsterdam, upon its passing into the possession of the Dutch. It is considered the oldest European settlement on the Delaware. Its situation, about half-way between Philadelphia and the sea, is evidently very advantageous, and must insure it a large share of the commercial prosperity of the capital. It may be safely predicted that its population will increase more during the next twenty years than in the one hundred and fifty which have elapsed since its establishment.

A few miles higher we saw, also on our left, the large town of Wilmington, pleasantly situated on an eminence, at some distance from the river, but commanding apparently a view of every sail passing upon it. I understood that it was the largest town of the Delaware State. We next came to Marcus Hook (also on the western shore); to a succession of low islands; to the mouth of the Schuylkyl, with Fort Miffin opposite to it, on the Jersey side, and soon after discovered Philadelphia itself, situated on the right or western bank of the Delaware. Though not presenting the splendor, nor majesty, nor venerable antiquity of some cities I had seen, not exhibiting the palaces of Calcutta, nor the temples of Benares, nor the marble domes and minarets of Agra and Delhi, its appearance was most gratifying to me as the city founded by Penn, as the seat of the American Government, and the termination of my voyage. Having passed several ships, the *India* entered the line and took her station along one of the wharves, which extended nearly the whole length of the city, and in a few minutes I *stepped ashore* without even the aid of a plank, the ship's side touching the wharf.

It being evening, when many people were about, the quay was crowded with persons curious to witness an arrival from Bengal. Having first gratified my own curiosity by looking at the lookers-on, and made a few turns up and down the wharf, enjoying the great pleasure of treading once more on firm ground after a long confinement to a ship, I was setting off with my trunk to a tavern when Mr. Pringle, the purser, stopped me with a pressing invitation to accompany him to the house of Mr. Lewis, one of the owners of the *India*.

This worthy citizen received me very kindly, saying, "How dost thou do, friend? I am glad to see thee;" for he was, in the phraseology of Philadelphia, one of the Society of Friends, that is to say, a Quaker. He introduced me to Mrs. Lewis and his daughters, who received me with the same salutation, "I am glad to see thee, friend; I hope thou art well." I drank tea with these good people, in whom I found a kindness which the simplicity of their manners seemed to make the more cordial. The safe arrival of their ship at a favorable market put all the family in good spirits. After tea I went to the house of Mr. Bingham, intending to go afterwards to the London Tavern, but Mrs. Lewis insisted upon my returning to sleep at her house: "Thou wilt sleep here, friend; thy bed shall be ready for thee." Mr. Bingham, to whom Mr. Pringle introduced me, was the principal person in Philadelphia, and the wealthiest, probably, in the Union. His house stood alone, and occupied, with the gardens attached to it, a spacious piece of ground. It was by far the handsomest residence in the city. I found here a large party. Besides Mr. and Mrs. Bingham and their two daughters, were Count de Noailles, Count Tilley, Mr. Alexander Baring, and others, After supper I returned to the house of Mr. Lewis, and was conducted to a handsome chamber, the centre of which was occupied by a square bed, with curtains all round it, in the English manner. There could not be a fairer promise of a good night's rest. After, however, I had slept an hour, I heard a person undressing behind the curtains, although there was no other bed in the room than that which I had supposed to belong exclusively to me. But this opinion was soon changed, for the stranger, having put out the light, drew back the curtains, and placed himself at my side. Sleeping ill with another person even in the same *room*, I would much rather have had Mrs. Lewis's bed, ample as it was, to myself; but I inferred that the arrangement which had taken place was one of the peculiar customs of the country, and that in America, when a stranger was invited to pass the night with his host, it was never meant to give him the whole of a bed. When the light of the morning shone upon the features of my companion, whose face should I see but Mr. Pringle's. Though surprised to find that the purser had slept so near me, I felt that I could not reasonably complain, for as his attentions had procured me this bed, no one certainly had so fair a claim to half of it as himself.

8th.—The next morning after breakfast I took a lodging at the principal hotel in Philadelphia, called the London Tavern, but found it so deficient in comfort that I sallied forth in search of better quarters. I asked a person in the street where the Members of Congress put up when they arrived from the different States, and was told that many of them lived together in a house in Fourth Street kept by an old Frenchman named Francis. I thought it would be very desirable to be admitted into this house, or rather into this society. I accordingly walked immediately to Fourth Street, and found old Mr. Francis and his American wife sitting together in a small dark room at the end of the passage. I did not at first know who Mrs. Francis was, for she appeared too tall and handsome to be the old man's daughter, and too young to be his wife. Mr. Francis, who seemed to have lost the politeness of his own country, said, without stirring from his chair, or scarcely raising his head, that his house was not a tavern, but a private house for the reception of Members of Congress, of whom it was now full. I mentioned that I was a stranger in America, being just arrived from the East Indies. The little old man regarded me with a look of surprise as I said this, but repeated, in a tone of diminished repugnance almost amounting to civil regret, that his house was full. I was about to return to my indifferent lodging at the London Tavern, when Mrs. Francis reminded her husband of a small room at the top of the house, which I might occupy for a day or two, when a chamber next to the one occupied by the Vice-President would be disengaged. The mention of the Vice-President excited my attention, and the idea of being placed so near him at once obtained my assent to Mrs. Francis's proposal; and the old man also expressed his concurrence, or rather allowed his wife to make what arrangement she pleased. I immediately brought my trunk from the London Tavern and placed it in my temporary apartment. I observed that the maid-servant who assisted in getting it up a steep and narrow staircase was a negress, or rather, a mulatto, the first human being of this race that I had seen. She was young, active, and obliging, and spoke English. She was the *property*, I understood, of Mr. Francis, who had *bought* her some time before, and might of course *sell* her whenever he pleased. This was the first instance of slavery I had ever seen, and it caused me both pain and surprise to meet with it in the country which so boasted of the freedom of its institutions.

At dinner to-day I met several members of the two Houses of Congress, and thought them most amiable, sensible men. The seat at the head of the table was reserved for the Vice-President, Mr. Adams, but he did not come to dinner. In the evening Mrs. Francis made tea for nearly the same party. Considering that I had arrived in America only the day before, that I had no introduction to any one, that there was not a good hotel in the city, and that the general usages of the country did not, as in India, supply this deficiency, I thought myself fortunate in being already established in the most respectable society of the United States. Mr. Bingham, the President of the Pennsylvanian State, not only gave me a general invitation to his house, but offered to take care of my great sheep during my stay in America. This fine animal had arrived in perfect health, as had my Santipore cow; but my Cachmirean goat, which was very sickly when we left India, had died shortly before we reached the Delaware.

The negress being engaged in arranging my chamber, my curiosity to see an American play led me to the theatre. The play was the "Miser," followed by the "Jubilee." I took my place in the front boxes, paying nearly the same price as in England.

9th April.—I breakfasted this morning at the public table, at which Madame Francis presided. Several members of both Houses were present. Mrs. Francis helped me to some of the celebrated buckwheat cakes, whose excellence had been the subject of much commendation during our voyage. It takes its name from the species of wheat of which it is made, and in size and appearance resembles the English crumpet, and is dressed in the same manner, being first toasted and then buttered. But it is superior to the crumpet or muffin, having the peculiar taste of the buckwheat, which is extremely agreeable, and renders it the most esteemed article of an American breakfast. This meal was, in other respects, very abundant and sumptuous, comprising tea, coffee, hot rolls, toast, eggs, ham, and joints of cold meat. It appeared the English breakfast of former days, with tea and its accompaniments added to it.

After this I called at Mr. Bingham's, where I found my doombah grazing upon the garden lawn at the back of the house. While I was looking at it with Mr. Bingham, several inhabitants of the city came to gratify their curiosity, for Mr. Bingham, having observed this, had ordered that everybody should be admitted, and considerable numbers had already come to the garden in consequence. My Bengal cow, which I found in a stable not far off, also had numerous visitors. Among the curiosities which I brought from India was an oyster-shell of extraordinary size and weight, exceeding one hundred pounds. It was the bottom shell alone, and had been found amongst a heap of oyster-shells at Madras. The mark of the oyster was visible upon the discolored surface of the inside, and showed that the fish had nearly filled the entire cavity. This curiosity I presented to the National Museum, where it was very graciously accepted.

I called upon Mr. Bond, the British Consul and temporary representative of the British Government in the absence of the Envoy. He asked me many questions about India, and said he must introduce me to General Washington. He invited me to spend that evening with him.

On returning to my lodging in Fourth Street, I found the negro girl bringing my things down-stairs from the garret. She told me, with much pleasure, that she was taking them to a room on the first floor, which her mistress had ordered for me. This I found to be a very good chamber, with two windows looking into a court behind the house. In a room adjoining, and nearly similar, was Mr. Adams, the Vice-President of the United States.

Soon after I was installed in my new quarters, Mr. Alexander Baring and his brother, Mr. Henry Baring, called upon me. I thought the former a clever, well-informed young man.* He was, I understood, come to America on account of Messrs. Hope's house, of Amsterdam, to purchase a large tract of land in the province of Maine, belonging to Mr. Bingham. I knew his brother in Bengal, the eldest son of Sir Francis Baring. He had married one of my fellow-passengers in the *Ponsborne*, granddaughter of Captain Thornhill.

I dined to-day with the Members of Congress. Mr. Adams took the chair always reserved for him at the head of the table,

---

* My acquaintance with Mr. A. Baring, now Lord Ashburton, has since been kept up. He always refers to our first meetings with much apparent satisfaction.

though himself superior to all sense of superiority. He appeared to be about sixty years of age. In person he was rather short and thick; in his manner somewhat cold and reserved, as the citizens of Massachusetts, his native state, are said generally to be. His presence caused a general feeling of respect, but the modesty of his demeanor and the tolerance of his opinions excluded all inconvenient restraint. He was generally dressed in a light or drab-colored coat, and had the appearance rather of an English country gentleman who had seen little of the world, than of a statesman who had seen so much of public life. He began his career at the bar of the Royal Courts of Boston, where he was said to have gained popularity by his eloquence, and esteem by his integrity and independence; but it is probable that the great powers of his mind, like those of Washington and other patriots, would have remained unknown if the Revolution had not brought them into notice. He was chosen by his countrymen to represent them in the first National Congress assembled at Philadelphia in the year 1774, the year before the commencement of open hostilities by the battle of Bunker's Hill, and during the war which followed he was associated with Franklin in the mission of the latter to the court of France. He was also employed in diplomatic negotiations with England and Holland. I was told that the troubles of his country had drawn from his pen some publications, in which his patriotism and his talents were equally conspicuous. Knowing few greater pleasures than that of listening to the conversation of great and virtuous men, I was always glad when I saw Mr. Adams enter the room and take his place at our table. Indeed, to behold this distinguished man, the future President of his country, occupying the chair of the Senate in the morning, and afterwards walking home through the streets and taking his seat amongst his fellow-citizens, as their equal, conversing amicably with men over whom he had just presided, and perhaps checked and admonished, was a singular spectacle, and a striking exemplification of the state of society in America at this period.

I drank tea, and spent the evening, with the English *chargé d'affaires*. There was a large party of ladies and gentlemen, all Americans. The reception was in a large room up-stairs, resembling in every respect an English drawing-room. The company sat round a wood-fire, placed in a shining grate. In the middle of the circle, after tea and coffee had been served round, figured the Consul himself, descanting on various subjects, public and private, as well as public and private characters, sometimes with unbecoming levity, sometimes with sarcasm still more unbecoming. The opinions he expressed could hardly fail to be offensive to the sentiments of many of his guests, and to the good taste of all. I was surprised at behavior so undignified, and felt some shame at seeing the representative of my country playing the part of a political mountebank before many of the principal persons of the American metropolis.

Sunday, 10th April.—I went this forenoon to hear the celebrated Dr. Priestley preach. The chapel, though spacious, was so crowded that I was obliged to stand near the door, and could only judge of the Doctor's eloquence by the pleasure it seemed to afford his hearers.

I dined and drank tea with Mr. Bingham, met the Count de Noailles, Count Tilley, the celebrated Monsr. Volney, the two Messrs. Barings, and several members of the Senate and House of Representatives—in all a very large party. Mr. Volney, next whom I sat at dinner, was very inquisitive about India. Mr. Alexander Baring, who sat nearly opposite to me, took a leading part in the general conversation. After tea, the Count de Noailles undertook to introduce me to Dr. Ross, an English physician, who would, he said, have much pleasure in seeing me. The Doctor, it appeared, was distinguished rather as a literary character than as a physician, not *practising* as such, though giving his gratuitous assistance to his countrymen and friends. This introduction proved very agreeable, and confirmed the favorable accounts I had received of the Doctor from the Count and others.

Monday, 11th.—Called this morning upon the Barings. Found them fencing together. After my return home I received a visit from Mr. Bond. He called to let me know that General Washington would hold a levee the next day, when he would introduce me to him. He said he would call upon me and take me with him, and begged me to be ready at the time fixed. Dr. Ross also called upon me, and was extremely civil. He invited me to dine with him the next day. Dined with the Vice-President and Members of Congress. In the evening went to the play, "All in the Wrong."

Tuesday.—After partaking of Mrs. Francis's buckwheat cakes, I put my head into the hands of the hairdresser. I had still preserved in its original length and fulness the *pigtail*, as it was called, with which I had left England, the democratic *crop* of the French Revolution not having yet reached India. I doubted, indeed, whether *style* of dress was required by the forms of the republican court at which I was about to appear; but as much of the attention I received seemed to be on account of my coming from India, I thought it as well to be presented in the costume of an Indian court. When dressed, I joined the Members of Congress in the public room, to wait for Mr. Bond. While conversing with these gentlemen, expecting the British *chargé* every minute, the negress entered, and delivered to me a note from this officer to say that important public business had suddenly made it impossible for him to attend the levee that day. I regretted this circumstance the more, because I was likely to leave Philadelphia before the next levee.

Scarcely had I resumed my common dress before Dr. Ross called. He said that, knowing that Dr. Priestley would be glad to see me, he called to accompany me to him. Disappointed of seeing one great man that morning, I considered myself fortunate in being thus introduced to another. I willingly, therefore, accepted the Doctor's obliging offer, and set out with him for Dr. Priestley's house in High Street.

High Street is considered the principal street in Philadelphia, although Broad Street, which crosses it towards its upper end, exceeds it somewhat in width. It runs perpendicularly from the river, or from east to west, and divides the city into two parts, nearly equal. The streets, which run in the line of the river, or from north to south, all cut High Street, and, of course, all the streets parallel to it, at right angles. The width of High Street is one hundred feet; that of all the others, with the exception of Broad Street, about fifty. All the streets being equidistant from each other, it is evident that their intersection forms the houses comprised between them into square masses of equal dimensions. Such is the simple but monotonous plan of Philadelphia, as laid down by its founder, William Penn, towards the end of the seventeenth century. The streets resemble many of the smaller streets of London, excepting that the foot-pavement on each side is of brick instead of stone. The houses also are built with red brick, and have generally a shop on the first floor, and two or three windows in the stories above. The streets and houses thus resembling each other, having scarcely any difference in their appearance, excepting the accidental dissimilarity arising from the shops, produces a sameness wearying to the eye, and often embarrassing to a stranger, who can hardly tell, when it is too dusk to read the names at the corners, whether he is in "Third" or "Fourth Street," "Chesnut" or "Walnut." For the nomenclature adopted by old Penn when he made his streets was as unusual as many other parts of his plan, and by aiming at extreme simplicity, produced eccentricity rather than convenience, confusion rather than clearness. Thus, the first street from the Delaware was called "First Street"; the succeeding ones "Second," "Third," "Fourth," "Fifth," "Sixth," and so on, as far as Broad Street, half way between the Delaware and the Schuylkyl. Beyond this line they were numbered in a similar way from the latter river towards the Delaware, the streets of the same number on the two sides of the line of separation being distinguished by the name of the *river* to which they belonged, as "Delaware First Street," "Schuylkyl First Street," "Delaware Fifth Street," "Schuylkyl Fifth Street," etc. This inconvenient arrangement seems to have been adopted on the supposition that the two sides of the city would be constructed simultaneously from the respective water fronts. This, however, was not the case; for the Delaware, offering much greater facilities for navigation, the city has been extended far beyond its intended limits, along the banks of this river, north and south, while no buildings have been commenced on the banks of the Schuylkyl to the present time (1796). Some streets, however, have been begun on the Schuylkyl side of Broad Street; and there can be no doubt that they will, in a few years more, reach that river. Whenever that may be the case, the inconvenience of having two sets of streets bearing the same names will probably be manifest, and may lead to a change less repugnant to custom and good taste. It is harsh enough for a stranger's ear to hear "Thirteenth Street" (the last next the midway division), without the distinction of "Delaware Thirteenth Street," or "Delaware Thirteenth," which will be necessary when the remaining or Schuylkyl half of the city shall be built. The names given to the other streets, those which run from the Delaware towards the Schuylkyl, are scarcely less whimsical, the principal *trees* of America having been chosen for this purpose, and thus forming Chesnut, Walnut, Pine, Cedar, Mulberry, Spruce, *Sassafras* streets. The distance between the two rivers is about two miles, over a level plain.

Proceeded to Dr. Priestley's house in the upper part of High Street, in a row of small houses between Sixth and Seventh streets, remarkable for their pleasant appearance, standing back a few yards from the footpath, and having small gardens, separated by painted rails, before them. I had not seen such an appearance of neatness and comfort since my arrival in Philadelphia, and experienced pleasure in finding that it was here that the English philosopher, the benefactor of his country and of mankind, by his discoveries in useful science, had taken up his abode. Having passed through the garden of one of the first houses, the door was soon opened by a female servant, who, saying that the Doctor was at home, conducted us into a small room by the side of the passage, looking towards the street. Here I expected to see the Doctor, but found only his sister, who desired the maid to let her master know that Dr. Ross was come. In a few minutes the Doctor, having quitted, probably, his studies, entered the room, and I was at once relieved from the sort of uneasiness which precedes an introduction to a great man, his countenance being exceedingly mild and good-natured, and his manner no less easy and conciliating. His person, short and slender, his age, apparently about sixty, and his unaffected cheerfulness at once reminded me of my Uncle Thomas—an impression that increased during the remainder of my visit.

Dr. Ross, in his friendly zeal, introduced me somewhat in the style of a showman at a country fair: "Mr. Twining—just arrived from Bengal—a great traveller on the Ganges—has been received by the Great Moghol," etc. The Doctor, his simplicity unchanged by this recital, received me with hearty kindness. He placed me near the fire, and took a chair by my side. I soon found that he was as inquisitive as Dr. Ross had represented him to be. Fortunately his inquiries were directed to such subjects respecting India as were familiar to me, such as the castes, customs, and character of the inhabitants; climate, productions, etc. Passing from general to particular questions, he wished to have a description of the couvre-capelle; and the numbers of this deadly snake which I had seen at Santipore enabled me to gratify his curiosity upon this point. I described also the mungoos, and the battle which I had seen between this animal and a couvre-capelle. He asked me about a particular fish, and about a particular property it possessed. I fortunately knew this, had *eaten* it, and remarked the peculiarity he alluded to.

The Doctor related, in his turn, many anecdotes, here further reminding me, by his playfulness and good-humor, of my learned uncle. He had a way, when telling his stories, of asking you to *guess* how a thing happened, saying, "Now, sir, how do you think this was?" waiting a few moments for an answer. Among other things, he spoke of the great sheep in Mr. Bingham's garden, expressing his intention of seeing it, and then alluded to the great improvement lately made by Mr. Bakewell of Leicestershire in the breed and management of animals. He said he once visited Mr. Bakewell, who showed him his improved race of sheep, and his fine bulls, remarkable for their size and symmetry. He saw two of these animals grazing peaceably in the same pasture. "I can," said Mr. Bakewell, "immediately make these bulls as furious as they are now quiet, and again make them friends." "And how," said the Doctor, addressing himself to me, "how, sir, do you think this was done? Why, sir, Mr. Bakewell ordered one of his men to drive a cow into the field, and the two bulls rushed at each other, and fought with the greatest fierceness. While they were thus engaged, the cow was driven out of the field, and the two champions grazed together quietly as before."

The Doctor having expressed a desire to see the skin of my shawl goat, it was settled that he would call the next day, and accompany me on board the *India*. I now took leave, much gratified with this personal introduction to a celebrated man, of whom I had heard a great deal when a boy at school; his system of chemistry—his phlogiston and anti-phlogiston and fixed air—then making much noise, and leading to various experiments upon balloons, etc., in which boys at that time, and I amongst others, took a part.

Upon separating from Dr. Ross I went to the house where the Congress held its meetings, situated in Chesnut Street. It is a large and handsome building, occupying the area of an extensive court, by the side of the street. Two folding-doors, accessible to everybody, led me at once into the hall of the National Representatives, who were then sitting, and engaged in debate. I stood in the space reserved for strangers, between the entrance and the low partition which separates it from the part occupied by the members. This space was small, and without seats. I was surprised to find so little accommodation for the public, in a country where the public was supposed to be especially considered. There might possibly be more room allotted to strangers in another part of the hall, but I did not observe any visitors, excepting such as stood near me. These being but few, I was able to advance at once to the partition. From this point I had an uninterrupted view of every part of the hall—I may say, of every member of the Assembly, for one of the advantages of this handsome room is, that the whole of it is visible from every part.

The subject of debate, when I entered, was the budget, and Mr. Gallatin was speaking. Mr. Gallatin is a native of France or Switzerland, but had long resided in America, and was now a naturalized citizen of the Republic. He was one of the principal members of the opposition, or of the anti-federal or democratic party, as opposed to the federal system, of which General Washington was the head. Although a slow and rather embarrassed delivery, as well as a peculiarity of accent, showed that Mr. Gallatin did not speak his native language, his speech discovered great acuteness, and the deep knowledge of the finances of the United States for which he was especially distinguished. His strong opposition to the measures of Government, and his democratical opinions, had lately drawn upon him the quills of Peter Porcupine, a satiric writer, who at this time attracted much attention in America by his opposition, in a popular, sarcastic style, to the opposers of the existing Constitution. This writer, however, was not an American subject, but the Englishman who has since been so much less advantageously known, in his own country, by his real name of William Cobbett. Mr. Gallatin was only three or four yards to the right of where I stood. His profile from this point, the thin, sharp outline of a Frenchman's face, his inclined attitude towards the President as he addressed him, and the slow perpendicular movement of his right arm, "sawing the air," formed a portrait which the occasional appearance of his name in public affairs always brings to my remembrance. Mr. Maddison, an eloquent and much-respected member, also spoke from his seat, a little to the right of the President; and Mr. William Smith, member for Baltimore, one of our party in Fourth Street, who defended the measures of Government, repelling the animadversions of Mr. Gallatin with much wit and severity. I recollect a few of his sarcastic phrases.

From the hall of the Representatives, I went to that of the Senate, or Upper Chamber, analogous, in its position in the state, to the British House of Peers. Mr. Adams, as Vice-President of the United States, presided over this assembly. He was seated in a raised recess on one side of the hall, which was oblong, and much smaller than that of the Representatives. The public was admitted to a raised gallery, which extended the whole length of the side opposite the President. Here, also, I heard some good speaking, though the chief orators are in the other chamber. In both assemblies the members had desks before them, on which they took notes, and laid their papers; but their speeches were extempore.

I dined with Dr. Ross. He received me in his study, up a very narrow staircase. The walls of the room were entirely covered with books. The Doctor introduced me to Mr. Woolstencraft, related to the authoress of that name, to Dr. or Mr. Boulman, a distinguished Irishman, and to Mr. Cooper, a young American who had recently made himself known by his writings. Mr. Dallas, an eminent English barrister, was expected, but sent a note to say he was prevented from coming. Dinner being ready, we descended to a room under the study. Mr. Cooper and the Doctor's other guests asked many questions about the Hindoos, the Ganges, the cities and monuments I had seen in the northern parts of my tour, and the languages. The Doctor's announcement that I spoke three languages of India, though there was nothing extraordinary in the fact, seemed to cause some surprise. After dinner Mr. Dallas came. He expressed particular interest about India, in which country some of his family had resided. It was late in the evening before this party, containing some of the most clever men in Philadelphia, broke up. Although I had experienced some disappointment in not being introduced to General Washington in the morning, I had, through the polite attentions of Dr. Ross, passed a most pleasant day.

12th April.—Breakfasted, as usual, with the Members of Congress, with whom I was now upon easy terms. As we stood round the fire, one of these gentlemen, Mr. Gallatin, examined the ends of my muslin neckcloth, and much surprise was expressed when I mentioned the cost at Santipore. Many questions were asked me respecting the qualities and prices of the fabrics of India, and it is not impossible that the lowness of the latter suggested the idea of a profitable speculation, the object of almost every American at this period.

The Vice-President always breakfasted in his own room. He had brought a man-servant with him from Boston, but the negress had the care of his chamber. This poor girl, being the only servant in the house, served everybody and did everything. Her activity and cheerful diligence were surprising.

In the forenoon Dr. Priestley called. He was accompanied by his son, who also had a desire to see the skin of my shawl goat. I accordingly set out with the great chemist and his son Joseph. We continued along Fourth Street till we came to Orchard Street, one of the streets perpendicular to the Delaware, and turning down it, arrived at the wharf at which the *India* was discharging her cargo. The Doctor noticed the skin of my poor goat with much interest, turning back the long hair and examining the downy wool beneath with much attention. He seemed to have been previously impressed with the common belief that the cashmere shawl was made from the ordinary wool of a particular race of sheep, and not from the remarkable substance he now saw, or the produce of a goat. The Doctor, being a zealous searcher of truth and fact, was evidently gratified with this discovery; while, having failed in my attempt to take the demonstration of an important problem to my own country, it was gratifying to me to be able to communicate it to the chief naturalist of America. I thought I could not dispose of this curiosity better than by placing it in his possession. I accordingly requested the Doctor to allow one of the sailors to carry it to his house. Although he yielded to this proposal with reluctance, I had the satisfaction of perceiving that it afforded him pleasure.

As we returned through the city I was desirous of learning if the Doctor was satisfied with his situation in a country which possessed no man eminent for science since the days of Franklin. He expressed himself satisfied with the attention he had received from the American Government, which had offered him the professorship of chemistry. He spoke with regard of Dr. Ross, whose society apparently best supplied the loss of Franklin, of Bishop Watson, and Doctors Parr and Price, the friends of the Doctor's earlier life. But it was evident that his satisfaction with America, which had received him, had not effaced his attachment to his native country, which had banished him. For Dr. Priestley, diverted unfortunately from his philosophical pursuits by the French Revolution, became by his imprudence one of the victims of that unsparing explosion.

Quitting the paths of science, he engaged in the political and metaphysical discussions of that troubled period, and was soon swept away by the violence of a storm which, but for this needless exposure, would have passed over him. The infuriated mob of Birmingham, a place fostered by practical science and enriched by the useful arts, broke into his house, pillaged his extensive library, burnt his valuable manuscripts and the notes of his unpublished observations, and destroyed his philosophical apparatus. These lamentable acts determined the Doctor to retire to America. Still, it was so evidently his desire to return to England whenever the passions of the moment should have subsided, that I determined to ascertain on my arrival in London how far such a step would be expedient.

13th April.—Hearing that the *Vermont* was about to sail for England, I write by her to my father. Wishing to see a few of the other principal cities of America, as well as something of the country, I decided upon an excursion as far as Baltimore, south of Philadelphia, and eventually to Washington, the contemplated metropolis of the United States, situated on the Potomac. At the latter place

I should find an East-Indian, Mr. Law, formerly of the Bengal Civil Establishment. Returning to England, the want of occupation there induced him to visit America. At that time the plan of building a new metropolis, to bear the name of Washington, was under consideration, and excited much speculation. Mr. Law had become acquainted with one of the proprietors of the land selected for the site of the new city, and confiding in an Act of Congress already passed for the transfer of the seat of government, had made a considerable purchase of ground from this person. It was, however, considered an adventure of much risk, for doubt was entertained not only whether, in case of General Washington's death, the proposed change would take place, but whether the removal of the seat of government would carry with it the augmentation of commerce and population which Mr. Law anticipated, and which was essential to the success of his speculation. I this afternoon took my place in the stage-wagon for Baltimore for the following morning.

14th.—At ten this morning the negro girl took my portmanteau under her arm, and accompanied me to the mail-wagon office. At half-past ten the wagon started up High

Street, passing before the window of Dr. Priestley. The vehicle was a long car with four benches. Three of these in the interior held nine passengers, and a tenth passenger was seated by the side of the driver on the front bench. A light roof was supported by eight slender pillars, four on each side. Three large leather curtains suspended to the roof, one at each side and the third behind, were rolled up or lowered at the pleasure of the passengers. There was no place nor space for luggage, each person being expected to stow his things as he could under his seat or legs. The entrance was in front, over the driver's bench. Of course the three passengers on the back seat were obliged to crawl across all the other benches to get to their places. There were no *backs* to the benches to support and relieve us during a rough and fatiguing journey over a newly and ill made road. It would be unreasonable to expect perfection in the arrangements of a new country; but though this rude conveyance was not without its advantages, and was really more suitable to the existing state of American roads than an English stage-coach would have been, it might have been rendered more convenient in some respects without much additional expense. Thus a mere strap behind the seats would have been a great comfort, and the ponderous leather curtains, which extended the whole length of the wagon, would have been much more convenient *divided* into two or three parts, and with a glass, however small, in each division to give light to the passengers in bad weather, and enable them to have a glimpse of the country. The disposal of the luggage also was extremely incommodious, not only to the owner, but to his neighbors.

We were quite full, having ten passengers besides the driver. Upon leaving the city we entered immediately upon the country, the transition from streets to fields being abrupt, and not rendered gradual by detached houses and villas, as in the vicinity of London. The fields, however, had nothing pleasing about them, being crossed and separated by the numerous intersections of the intended streets, and surrounded by large rough-hewed rails, placed zigzag, instead of hedges. We soon reached the Schuylkyl, a small river which descends from the Kittatany mountains, in the back part of Pennsylvania, and enters the Delaware seven miles below Philadelphia, after a course of about 120 miles.

We crossed it upon a floating bridge, constructed of logs of wood placed by the side of each other upon the surface of the water, and planks nailed across them. Although this bridge *floated* when not charged, or charged but lightly, the weight of our wagon depressed it several inches below the surface, the horses splashing through the water, so that a foot-passenger passing at the same time would have been exposed to serious inconvenience. The roughness and imperfection of this construction on the principal line of road in America, and not a mile from the seat of government, afforded the most striking instance I had yet seen of the little progress the country had hitherto made in the improvements of civilization. The existence of such a bridge seemed the more surprising, as it completely obstructed the navigation of the river, which would otherwise, I was told, admit small craft as high as Reading, nearly eighty miles further up. I mention this instance of backwardness, and other deficiencies of a similar kind, not as a reproach to America, but as singular facts, exemplifying the difficulties and necessarily slow advancement of a new country. I believe there is no nation that would have done more in so short a time, and most nations would assuredly have done infinitely less. The transplanted branch of the British oak had already taken root, and displayed the vigor and strength of the parent stock. It was flattering to an Englishman to see the intelligence, energy, and enterprise which were manifest. Everywhere the progress of improvement was visible; everything had advanced, and was advancing. The bridge of planks and logs had probably succeeded a more insecure boat, and would certainly in a few years be replaced by arches of brick or stone.

The sloping banks of the Schuylkyl appeared to offer delightful situations for villas and country-houses, whenever the wealth and taste of the citizens of Philadelphia should lead them to the imitation of European indulgence, unless the extension of the city to the river should cover its borders with wharfs and warehouses, thus realizing the original design of William Penn.

A little beyond the bridge we came to a turnpike gate, the first I had seen since leaving England. It was interesting on this account, and further so, as showing that America had adopted a custom of the mother country which Adam Smith cites as one of the most equitable examples of taxation, the traveller paying for an evident convenience and in proportion as he enjoys it. It was probable that the tax collected here, or a part of it, was employed in securing the logs and planks of the bridge, or in replacing such as were carried away by the current— an accident which seemed likely to occur frequently.

The country now became hilly in some degree, and from the days of my journey in Scotland I was fond of hills. These were neither long nor high, but they presented some steep declivities, down which the wagon descended at a great rate, for not only was it unprovided with a drag to keep it back, but it seemed to be the principle of American driving to go as fast as possible downhill in order to make up for the slowness inevitable on all other parts of the road. This road being newly and roughly formed, furrowed with ruts, and strewed with large stones which had been separated from the mould or gravel, the jolting of the wagon in these rapid descents was almost insupportable, and even drew forth many a hard exclamation from my companions, accustomed to it as they were. At first our rapidity on these occasions, with a steep declivity, without rail or fence of any sort on one side, seemed to be attended with no trifling degree of danger; but I soon found that the driver managed his four active little horses with all the skill of an English coachman, although he had little the appearance of one, having neither his hat on one side, nor his great-coat, nor his boots, but a coarse blue jacket, worsted stockings, and thick shoes.

When eight miles from Philadelphia we passed through the small village of Derby, and in about as many more reached Chester, the end of the first stage. An English traveller is at first surprised to find the villages, often clumps of houses, of America bearing the names of the great towns or cities of England, although the latter, probably, had a beginning equally unimportant and diminutive. The country we had passed through since leaving the Schuylkyl was, for the most part, cleared of its ancient woods, at least near the line of our road, and cultivation had commenced; but the surface of the land was entangled with the roots of trees, and covered with stones which the plough had recently exposed to the light for the first time, and with clods of earth not yet broken. All the enclosures were formed in the manner already described—that is, by rough bars or rails placed one above another in a zigzag direction. The few farm-houses visible were also formed by bars or logs of wood, covered with laths and plaster. The situation of the inhabitants of these sequestered dwellings did not appear very enviable, though it doubtless had its charms, or its recompense at least. Every first settler in a new country labors less for the present than for the future, for himself than for his posterity, and it is this honorable consciousness that invigorates his toil, cheers his solitude, and alleviates his privations.

As we rattled down a steep hill leading to Chester, I thought there was a fair chance of our ending the first stage at the bottom of a precipice on our left, and so we probably should if we had *missed stays;* but when within three or four feet of the edge, the driver went cleverly on the *other tack*, till brought up by the high bank on that side, when he again *put about*, and made for the precipice, and thus by great skill got us safe to the inn at the bottom.

Chester is a small town of no present importance; but its situation as the first post or stage between Philadelphia and the Southern States seemed to insure its progressive extension and prosperity. It was now chiefly interesting as the place where Penn, having landed at Newark with his Quakers, and the grant of Charles the Second, bestowing upon him the immense tract of country to which he here, perhaps, gave his name, held his first assembly, producing his authority, and explaining, it is probable, his views and intentions. It appears that some Indians still retained their possessions in this part of the country, and that their chiefs were received with kindness at this meeting, and with assurances of justice and protection. Although such assurances are generally made and seldom observed, one is willing to suppose that Mr. Penn promised no more than he meant to perform; but it is painful to consider that the Indian tribes, instead of being civilized and improved by this event, were gradually compelled to recede before the influx of European nations, carrying their original barbarism, with the admixture, perhaps, of new vices and disease, to other settlements in the interior, from which they were again dislodged as the tide of intrusion rolled on.

It is possible that the general outline of the State of Pennsylvania may have undergone some change since Penn enrolled his charter in the village of Chester in 1682; but I believe the limits were nearly then what they are now (1796), extending from the Delaware to the shores of the Ohio, and of Lakes Erie and Ontario — a vast extent of country to be granted to one individual, either on the ground of service rendered the State by the father of William Penn, or as a debt due to the latter by the crown. Of these two motives, the most interested one must, perhaps, be considered the most probable. We naturally wish to know what advantages Penn derived from his great acquisition, and are hardly surprised to learn that the affairs of his province involved him in innumerable disputes and difficulties, and even encroached upon his private fortune. He died in the year 1718 at the age of seventy-four. It is probable that his name is held in respect by the "Friends" of Pennsylvania; but I never heard it mentioned in general society, nor observed that it was common. There was no one who bore it, either in the national representation or in the provincial assemblies of the State.

As the extreme jolting of the wagon had caused a general complaint among the passengers, and the inconvenience might be expected to increase as we got further from the capital, I proposed to join two or three of the party in hiring some other conveyance, but found that the wagon was the only carriage on the road. Having therefore changed our horses for four others of the same small but excellent race, we resumed our seats upon the bare planks, and continued our journey. The reserve of a first stage being over, the passengers became rather clamorous. They were, however, most polite towards me, exempting me from their sallies and jokes. Their wit was particularly directed against a "*Yankee*" who was one of the company. *We* apply this designation as a term of ridicule or reproach to the inhabitants of all parts of the United States indiscriminately; but the Americans confine its application to their countrymen of the Northern or New England States, and more especially to those of Massachusetts.

Four miles from Chester we passed through a small hamlet called Chichester, and soon after quitted the fine province of Pennsylvania, and entered the small State of Delaware, forming a narrow slip along the right bank of the Delaware River to the sea. I had had a view of the whole length of its water boundary as I sailed up the Delaware in the *India*. The part of this little district which I now saw appeared to have a pleasant and healthy elevation; but the lower parts, towards the shore of the Atlantic, contain numerous fens or marshes called swamps. One of these, called the Cypress Swamp, is said to be twelve miles in length and six in breadth.

When about twelve miles from Chester, passing over some high land called the Heights of Christiania, we descended to a creek of that name, and soon after entered Wilmington, which I have already mentioned (in describing our passage up the Delaware) as the principal town of the Delaware State, although Dover is the seat of government —for what reason I do not know, unless because its position is more central, a very *good* reason, which is not so much attended to in the establishing of metropolitan towns as public convenience frequently requires.

Having again changed horses, we reached the Brandywine, a small stream which flows from the Welch Mountains, in the interior of Pennsylvania. The Brandywine mills, for grinding corn, are very celebrated, and their great neatness and flourishing activity had a very pleasing appearance from the road. Here America already exhibited a spot which might be compared with any similar scene in England. I saw some small craft, of apparently about ten or fifteen tons; but I understood that sloops of a much larger size could mount the stream from the Delaware. These mills were said to furnish a very considerable part of the best flour consumed in Philadelphia.

I was glad that my presence did not prevent my fellow-travellers from speaking with much enthusiasm of an action fought here, during the late war, between the American troops and the British forces under the command of General Clinton. I cannot find a note I have somewhere of the particulars of this engagement. But the American army, commanded by General Washington, defended the passage of the Brandywine with great bravery, and indeed with success, till outflanked and turned by Lord Cornwallis, who crossed the river higher up. The British troops advanced, and took possession of Philadelphia. It appeared to me that the banks of the Schuylkyl might have offered another point of defence, but they doubtless did not. Indeed, the situation of the American army might have been too critical, with the Delaware in its rear, unless it had been possible to secure its retreat by a bridge of boats across that river. But although the American capital was thus lost on the Brandywine, the Americans consider that day, so calamitous to their cause, as highly honorable to their arms. It is a circumstance creditable to the talents of a general, and to the generosity of the nation he serves, when he can sustain defeat without losing the esteem and confidence of his countrymen. It may also be considered one of the peculiarities of such contests between a disciplined army and irregular troops, that the latter often gain glory in defeat, while *victory* is hardly glorious to their opponent.

We next changed horses at Newark, and completed our day's journey, soon after sunset, at Head of Elk, the name given to a few houses situated upon the Elk River, which we crossed in a boat, hauling upon a rope stretched across it. Here again it was easy to contemplate a future bridge. It was not, as in India, where the surplus revenue of the country was sent out of it, without being counterbalanced by any return. Here, this surplus would be expended *in* the country, whose property indeed it was, in national improvements. America was a farm, in which the produce was spent upon the land; India, one in which even stubble was carried from it.

During the last stage we had passed the White and Red Clay creeks. At the latter, General Washington had attempted to make a stand against the royal army which the British fleet had brought from New York, and landed at the head of Chesapeak Bay, not far from the place where we now stopped for the night. After the roughest journey I had ever had, a good supper and bed would have been very acceptable, but nothing could well be worse than the provision made for the travellers in both these respects. After a sparing and ill-dressed repast, which drew forth bitter words, and *more* than words, from the Yankee and most of his countrymen, we were conducted, one following another, up a narrow staircase, little better than a ladder, and all, to my utter despair, shut in one room, upon whose floor—which, by-the-bye, appeared to have little benefited by its proximity to the waters of the Chesapeak—were placed a few rude, unfurnished bedsteads, without curtains, ranged one close to another, like cots in a soldiers' barrack. Whether, however, it was my very good-fortune, or the politeness of the Americans, whose attentions I had received along the road, I could not tell, but it so happened that in the distribution and coupling which took place I remained without a partner, being the only one, I believe, who had this invaluable privilege. I was so sensible of the advantage I had obtained that I should have been glad to enjoy it a little longer the next morning; but at half-past two the tawny girl (slave, I fear I might call her) who had lighted us up-stairs, reappeared with a candle in her hand, and announced that the wagon would soon be ready.

At three o'clock, with no other light than what was afforded by the twinkling of the stars, the wagon and everything it contained, the passengers *on* the hard seats, their portmanteaus *under* them, were once more literally *in motion*, for the road was far from improving as we advanced into the State of Maryland, which we had entered the preceding afternoon. Soon after leaving the inn we crossed another small stream, called Elk Creek. It is the union of this with the rivulet we had passed the evening before that forms the larger stream, at the head of which the foundations of a future town have been so judiciously laid. This spot, covered by the two streams whose junction opens a communication with the Chesapeak in front, would in Europe probably have been chosen for a military position. But such advantages, happily, did not enter into the calculations of the Americans, who, not having to intrench themselves against the jealousy or ambition of surrounding nations, directed their attention to situations the most favorable to the establishments of agriculture and commerce, of peace, and not of war. They chose a rivulet, not to defend a bastion, but to turn a mill.

We proceeded very slowly till break of day, and not very fast after, the road being exceedingly deep and rough, often quitting what appeared to be the intended line, and winding, for a fresh and firmer bottom, through the partially cleared forest on either side, the driver, with great dexterity, guiding his horses round the stumps of trees, going over such roots as would only shake us a little, and avoiding others that would be likely to overturn us. The fields of such parts as were cleared were always surrounded by the zigzag fence of bars. The planting of hedges had not yet commenced, all refinement in agriculture, as in other things, being reserved for a more advanced stage of society, when population should be more abundant, labor cheaper, and public taste more improved. It would, however, have been an easy and cheap embellishment of the country, if a few of the fine trees of the ancient forests had been allowed to remain, if not in the fields, at least in the line of the future hedgerows. But *all* the trees being cut down, about three feet above the ground, the openings left in the forests were extremely unpicturesque, the enclosures having the appearance of large sheep-pens. Although the remaining stumps of the trees rendered the fields most unsightly, and, obstructing the plough, obliged the farmer to leave much ground uncultivated, they would probably remain undisturbed until the decay of their roots should facilitate their removal. For in a new country, as America now was, land is cheap and labor dear; but as the nation advances towards maturity, the reverse becomes the case, labor growing abundant, and the value of the produce of the earth rising with the demands of an extended population. Perhaps the happiest point for a country is the medium between these extremities.

Soon after sunrise we crossed a river on which Charlestown is situated, two miles lower, at its junction with the Chesapeak, and at nine o'clock reached the banks of the Susquehannah, where we found a boat ready to take us over to Havre de Grace, on the opposite side. As we pulled upon the rope stretched across this rapid stream, I contemplated, with peculiar pleasure, the ancient woods which still threw their broad shadow upon its surface. I was greatly struck with the wild poetic cast of this enchanting spot, all the features of which were as Indian as its name, excepting, indeed, the new-built town of Havre de Grace, whose white houses on the southern shore had supplanted the wigwams of the Susquehannah tribes, and interrupted the magnificent line of foliage.

I could not but feel a great desire to remain longer amidst such scenery, and explore the further beauties which the course of the Susquehannah would probably disclose. This river, however, though one of the largest that run into the Chesapeak, is not of very great length, since its sources are in the Alleghany Mountains, in the upper parts of the States of Pennsylvania and New York, a distance of about three hundred miles. Although much obstructed, in this course, by falls and rapids, it is navigable, or, as the Americans say, *boatable*, down the stream, nearly from its rise; but sloops and sea-craft can ascend it only three or four miles above Havre, being there stopped by some rapids. It is not improbable that many of these impediments will hereafter be removed, or avoided by means of locks and canals and other contrivances, and that a navigable communication may connect the Chesapeak, the great Atlantic lake, with the chain of lakes in the north, and with the Ohio and Mohawk rivers, and thus by the Mississippi and Hudson, into which these rivers respectively flow, with New Orleans and New York. Such are the gigantic schemes of this aspiring people. It is, perhaps, not too much to say, that the nation which, even in the first years of its political existence, has the genius to form such projects, and the patriotism to dwell upon them with confidence and enthusiasm, has already established the probability of their execution. None of my companions had followed the banks of the Susquehannah, but I understood from them that its greatest beauties were at the passage of one of its branches through the Alleghany Mountains. Its width, on reaching the Chesapeak about two miles from Havre, was said to exceed a mile. I always experience great difficulty in judging of the width of rivers, but the Susquehannah, at our ferry, did not appear to me to be so broad as the Thames at Twickenham.

At the best inn I had yet seen in America, neat, clean, and pleasantly situated, we found a good and abundant breakfast ready for us, consisting of tea, coffee, eggs, and cold meat. Here seemed to be another instance of that degree of improvement to which everything, probably, was advancing, though often imperceptibly, and with uneven steps; and not with the premature precipitancy unreasonably expected by too many travellers from other countries.

Our next stage was to Harford Bush, a very small town, but pleasantly and advantageously situated upon an inlet of the Chesapeak, here about ten miles in width. In some parts of this noble bay, particularly below the junction of the Potomac, the width exceeds twenty miles. Its length, in a northerly direction, from Cape Henry in Virginia to the mouth of the Susquehannah, is nearly three hundred miles. Its depth, and the facility it offers to navigation, may be inferred from the circumstance, already mentioned, that the British fleet sailed up it and landed the army at its northern extremity, near the Head of Elk. It would be pleasing to imagine the extraordinary sight which such a fleet on the basin of the Chesapeak must have presented, if it could be detached from the lamentable cause connected with it. A citizen of the United States may, without much generosity, forgive injuries from which his country derives its being; but an Englishman can scarcely revert to the same acts without a painful sense of imprudence and injustice.

While the numerous bays and inlets of the Chesapeak and the streams which run into it on either side seemed favorable to commerce, its waters were said to afford excellent fish, and also the celebrated canvas-back duck, of which I had heard much on board the *India*, as well as since my arrival in America, without having yet had an opportunity of forming my own opinion of its merits.

Having changed horses at Harford Bush, we went on to Joppa, passing in our way the

Gunpowder River. Journeying over the same wild country, woods in their primitive state, or partially cleared, with now and then a log-house, the appearance of which, unsurrounded by society or resources, was more dismal than cheering, we came to the small hamlet of Kingsbury, and at four in the afternoon reached Baltimore.

We drove in good style into the court-yard of the "Indian Queen," a large inn of very respectable appearance. It formed one of the angles between Market and Queen streets, in the upper part of the town, and had an extensive front in each street.

I could not separate from my companions without taking leave of them all, and acknowledging the polite attentions they had shown me; for though a total want of reserve amongst themselves almost degenerated sometimes into coarseness, their behavior towards me was uniformly obliging. Soon after I had taken possession of my quarters, a small room with a very small bed, fronting, at my desire, the principal street, I was told that dinner was ready, and was shown into the largest room I had ever seen in any hotel even in England. It extended the whole depth of the house, from Queen Street to the great court-yard, and was divided along the middle by a broad fixed table, nearly as long as the room itself. I found a large party assembled, or assembling, consisting almost entirely of travellers and lodgers in the house, and not of residents in the town, for anti-Britannic as the Americans are in their political feelings, they have the domestic propensities of their ancestors, every man dining with his family, if he has one. After the dinner, which was composed principally of large joints of meat and dishes of vegetables, served more in abundance than variety, each person rose when he pleased and retired without ceremony, much as in India. I was glad to avail myself of this *freedom* in order to see something of Baltimore that evening.

I accordingly walked down the principal street, which had a gentle slope from the country, a little above the "Indian Queen," and turning when near the bottom of it to the right, through some smaller streets, came to the Port, an extensive basin formed by the Patapsco River, before it reaches the Chesapeak; or perhaps it may as reasonably be considered an *inlet* of the Chesapeak, into which the Patapsco discharges itself. I here saw many ships and sea-vessels of various descriptions. Some were in the stream, others against the wharfs which lined the shore, and there seemed room for a much larger number, the width of the basin appearing to me to be at least a mile, and its length towards the Chesapeak much more. The advantages of the position were so evident that it was not surprising it should have been early selected for the foundation of a commercial city. The Port seemed effectually defended by a small fort called Fort Henry. Unfortunately there is an insufficient depth of water close to the town, so that a ship with a full and heavy cargo on board cannot come alongside the wharfs, as the *India* did at Philadelphia. But this objection does not apply to a part a little lower down, called Fell's Point, where consequently many houses and warehouses are already built, and to which Baltimore is rapidly extending.

As I returned up the town by another street I passed by the house of Mr. Gilmore, whose son had made the voyage to Calcutta in the *India,* and returned with me in that ship. It was a large, square, detached mansion, the handsomest I had yet observed in Baltimore. I deferred calling upon young Mr. Gilmore till the next day. After strolling about till dark I returned to the "Indian Queen," and spent a little time in the great room before going to bed.

Sunday.—On returning to the public hall this morning I found several persons at breakfast at the long table, each in his own way. By the side of the room was a table plentifully charged with cold meat, to which most of the company seemed to have recourse. Some had hot beefsteaks. After breakfast I walked up Market Street, which, however, did not extend far in that direction, but the ground was marked for carrying the town further. The houses here were larger and handsomer in general than in the lower streets, but all were nearly upon the same plan, being built of red brick, having two or three windows in front, and three ranges of rooms or stories in height, of which the lowest was generally occupied by the shop and the passage, and the two above by sitting-rooms and bedrooms. The street was well paved, and had a good foot-pavement on each side. I walked through several other streets, nearly all of the same appearance, but not intersecting each other with the same symmetrical regularity as at Philadelphia. There was also a striking difference in the moral aspect of the two cities, Baltimore not having the dull uniformity which the dress and manners of a Quaker population gave to the metropolis.

I went into a church in one of the streets to the left of Market Street. It was a large, commodious building, with the exterior rather of a chapel, being built of red brick, and having neither tower nor steeple. The interior arrangement and the service were nearly those of an English church.

Soon after my return to the "Indian Queen," while preparing for my visit to Mr. Gilmore, I was informed that the Danish Consul had called to see me. I was surprised, having no knowledge of any one at Baltimore excepting young Mr. Gilmore. Upon going to the great room, where the Consul was waiting, this gentleman introduced himself to me as Mr. Barry, saying he had received a letter from Mr. Law of Washington, who had hoped to meet me himself at Baltimore, but not being able to set out so soon as he had expected, had written about me to him. When I announced to Mr. Law my intention of visiting him, I received a most polite and pressing invitation, but did not suppose he would carry his attentions further. Mr. Barry, whom I found a very gentlemanly man, was extremely civil, offering me, in the most friendly manner, his services during my stay in Baltimore.

When Mr. Barry had left me, I walked down the town to the house that had been pointed out to me, the evening before, as Mr. Gilmore's. My shipmate seemed very glad to see me again, and leaving me for two or three minutes, returned to the parlor with his father, Mrs. Gilmore, two sisters, and an elder and younger brother. All this fine family received me with as much attention as if I had rendered some essential service to Mr. W. Gilmore, which was by no means the case. The respectable old gentleman insisted upon my coming to dine with him that day, which I accordingly did, and passed the evening most agreeably, discovering no difference whatever between an American and an English fireside. On this occasion, as on many others, I found the information I had collected in different parts of India, respecting the manufactures and commerce of that country, very useful, inasmuch as it enabled me to make acceptable communications upon these subjects. By a commercial treaty lately concluded between Great Britain and the

United States, under the auspices of Lord Grenville and Mr. Jay, American ships were allowed to trade with the East India Company's possessions. The consequence was, that the American merchants had their attention at this time very much directed to this new and promising branch of commerce; and Mr. Gilmore, one of the principal merchants of Baltimore, and already holding a share in the *India*, was glad to be informed of the names, qualities, prices, and places of manufacture of such fabrics of the interior of India as were suited to the American market. Mr. Gilmore was surprised to find so great a difference between the original cost of many sorts of goods, and the prices exacted from the inexperience of American captains and supercargoes at Calcutta. I suggested a mode by which better assortments might be procured, at a reduction of ten per cent. on the prices now paid.

Monday.—I had not long returned to my own room after breakfast this morning before I was told that a gentleman had called upon me, and was waiting in the passage below. When I was within a few steps of the bottom of the stairs, a gentleman advanced hastily to meet me, and taking me warmly by the hand, said, "I am sure you are Mr. Thomas Twining, you are so like your father." This unceremonious stranger was Mr. Law, just arrived from Washington. I took him into a parlor on the ground floor, and there we had a long conversation about India, where he still had many friends. After a very pleasant interview, he invited me to dine with him that day, at Mr. Barry's, with whom he was staying : he would then, he said, introduce me to Mrs. Law, who had accompanied him from Washington.

Being unwell this forenoon, I was recommended to Dr. Jamieson, a physician, or rather an apothecary with that title, who lived a few doors above the "Indian Queen," on the opposite side of the way. He had a considerable reputation, and was, at least, a sensible, agreeable man. The circumstance of my coming from Bengal seemed to interest him much. I dined with the Danish Consul. Mr. Law introduced me to Mrs. Law, with whom I was much pleased. She was granddaughter of Mrs. Washington, the President's lady.

Tuesday.—Had a very friendly visit this morning from Dr. Jamieson, who expressed a wish to introduce me to his family. Called upon Mr. Law, and afterwards upon Mr. Gilmore.

Wednesday.—Mr. Gilmore and his son called this morning to let me know that the ship *Polly* was about to sail for Bengal. As soon as they had left me I wrote to the Resident of Santipore to inform him of my arrival in America; I had written to him from the banks of the Jumna; I now addressed him from those of the Patapsco. Two English gentlemen called upon me soon after I had finished my letter. They came, they said, at the desire of the St. George's Society at Baltimore, to request my company at their Anniversary dinner, the next day, it being St. George's day. Not long after these gentlemen had left me I received a visit from Mr. Law, who called to accompany me to Mr. Edward Thornton, the British Consul. Mr. Thornton received me with much politeness, and after some inquiries about India asked me if I was related to Mr. Daniel Twining, of Pembroke Hall, Cambridge. He said that he himself had formerly belonged to that College, and that he had, in consequence, still some claims upon it, to which his absence from England had prevented his attending. I said I should probably go to

Pembroke to see my brother, and would willingly deliver any letter or message to the master of the College. Mr. Thornton said he would give me a letter for the master, Dr. Turner.

At dinner to-day, at the great table, some travellers from Virginia sat opposite to me. Finding I had some intention of visiting that state, they jokingly advised me to be on my guard against the Virginian practice of *gouging*, by which a man dexterously forces out the eye of another with whom he quarrels. I expressed the difficulty I had in believing that this practice could be so common as the inhabitants of the Northern States represented it to be. One of the party observed that if I went as far as Alexandria, as I talked of doing, I should see persons who had lost an eye in the manner alluded to. Upon my observing that I could not conceive how this operation could be so easily accomplished, he said that if I wished it he would soon show me. Expressing my consent, he rose, and, walking round the end of the table, came towards me. Having seated myself a little way from the table, he placed himself before me, laid hold of the hair by the side of my head, and twisting his fingers well in it, brought his thumb to the corner of my eye, against which he pressed with a force, or rather with a *command*, that satisfied me of the *possibility* of removing an eye from the socket in this manner. When he had disentangled his fingers from my hair, and I was at liberty, there was a jocular expression of satisfaction amongst the company, and some gentlemen assured me afterwards that they were glad to see me safe out of the Virginian's hands.

There exists a hostile, or, at least, an unfriendly spirit between many of the States composing the American Union; but this sentiment is more intense and uncharitable, assuming almost the character of fixed antipathy, between the Northern and Southern States. It seemed, indeed, that the citizens of Massachusetts, and those of Georgia, Carolina, and Virginia are distinguishable by very opposite qualities. The inhabitants of the former are considered prudent, moral, diligent; but with more industry than genius. The native of Virginia is generous, improvident, choleric, eloquent; but manifesting in his pursuits more genius than morality or exertion. His general character seems to assimilate him more to a native of Ireland or of

France than of England, and the Virginian, who conceals not his repugnance to the English, from whom indeed his country experienced much violence during the war, would not perhaps object to this classification. But the chief and least-disputed reproach to which the inhabitants of the Southern States are liable, is that of dissipation, susceptibility of offence, and gambling. They are extremely fond of cock-fighting and other cruel sports, and their passion for gaming is said to be without restraint. In their frequent duels they sometimes fight with muskets, and in their common affrays they gouge and commit other barbarities. The character of the Middle States, New York, Pennsylvania, the Jerseys, and Maryland, seems to be a modification of the extremes which distinguish the provinces of the north and south. It would, however, be very unreasonable to consider such a geographical distribution of the virtues and defects of a nation as minutely correct; but this outline may perhaps possess sufficient resemblance to give some idea of the characteristic features which distinguish the moral physiognomy of certain sections of the United States.

23d April.—I this morning received a visit from the British Consul. In the afternoon I dined with the St. George's Society in the great room in which they held their meetings. I was received by the President and Vice-President, who introduced me to several members of the Society. Although the party was limited to English, Irish, and Scotch, the numbers filled a table which extended nearly the whole length of the room. The President, on taking the chair, placed me on his right hand, opposite Mr. Thornton, who sat on his left. After a very handsome dinner, the healths of the President of the United States and of the King of England, and other toasts, were drunk, intermixed with songs. After a very agreeable evening of patriotic and temperate festivity, I acknowledged the gratification I had received, and returned to my lodging before the party broke up.

When I was at Dehli the Great Moghol, wishing to express his satisfaction with some communications I had succeeded in making to him, allowed me, at my suggestion, to have his name and the date of my reception at his Court engraved on some personal ornament. Accordingly on my return to Bengal I had a small tablet of silver handsomely engraved with the Emperor's name in Persian characters, and the date of my introduction to him. Some years after, when in charge of an extensive district in the interior of India, and which, as it happened, had been the residence of His Majesty's predecessors on the throne, and the scene of his own early military exploits, I was in the habit of wearing this ornament upon receiving visits from the Rajah and other principal personages of the country. Desirous now of expressing my sense of the attentions I had received from my countrymen, I again wore this memorial, and presented it to the President and others, who examined it with curiosity, and were amused with the history belonging to it.

24th April.—Breakfasted, as usual, at the great table. In the forenoon Mr. Law and other friends called, and also a Mr. Field, an English miniature painter, who had dined with the St. George's Society the day before. He expressed a wish that I would *sit* to him, which I agreed to do on my return from Washington, for which I was to leave Baltimore in a day or two. Dined with Mr. Law at Mr. Barry's. In the evening Dr. Jamieson called, and stayed and supped with me.

25th.—Mr. and Mrs. Law set out in their chariot and four horses for Washington. I had not seen such an equipage in America. They invited me to accompany them, but besides my unwillingness to add to their inconvenience on the bad roads they had to travel, I had some engagements which prevented my leaving Baltimore till the next day. Much rain after Mr. Law's departure. Write to my brother by a ship bound to England.

26th.—At four this morning I quitted Baltimore, where I had passed a few days most agreeably, having found numerous friends where I expected to find none but strangers, and received a degree of spontaneous kindness and hospitality upon which I had still less reason to calculate.

In the stage-wagon, for such again was the conveyance, were ten other passengers. After going eight miles we reached the Patapsco, a small river which rises in the southern part of Pennsylvania. We crossed it in a boat which held the wagon and horses, the passengers remaining in their places, for the difficulty of getting in and out prevented our leaving these on trifling occasions, such as crossing a ferry, or stopping to change horses, or going up a hill.

At eight o'clock we reached a solitary inn called "Spurrier's," where we found the usual substantial American breakfast. The country through which we had passed was extremely dismal, being covered with forests upon which the axe had as yet made but little impression, for, excepting a few open spots here and there, such trees alone were cut down as were necessary for the formation of a road, or rather the *line* of a road, for this was still in a very rude state, the driver being obliged to wind as well as he could between the remaining stumps. The soft soil being rendered deep by the rain that had fallen, our progress was very slow, not exceeding thirteen miles in four hours—a pace slower than that to which I had been accustomed in my palanquin in India. My companions were chiefly from Virginia and the Southern States, and were very lively. They urged me to extend my travels to the south, but at the same time did not conceal the aversion of their countrymen towards the English nation, nor the caution this feeling would require me to adopt in my intercourse with the inhabitants.

Our next stage was to another solitary station called "Van's," fifteen miles; the whole, with very little exception, through thick woods. The wagon, in winding through the trees and over their roots, was often so depressed in the soft ground and old ruts on one side, that the passengers were obliged to press towards the other. Without this perpetual *trimming* we should certainly have been overturned; not that such an adventure would have been attended with any serious consequence, the wagon being so low, and the pace so slow: the scramble therefore on these occasions was attended with more mirth than apprehension. Eight miles more, over a country more cleared and a better road, brought us to the "Indian Queen" at Bladensburg, a small, solitary inn, surrounded by a few rude cottages, which a few years would probably transform into respectable houses, particularly if the new city, now distant only one stage, should become the seat of government.

While we were at dinner one of the party informed Mr. Ross, the civil landlord, that I came from Bengal. "Why," observed Mr. Ross, "the gentleman speaks English as we do."

Over the fireplace in the dining-room was a plan of Washington, with the streets, squares, and public buildings of the intended city minutely detailed.

Our next and last stage of twelve miles was pretty good as to road and country, but we had a great deal of rain, which obliged us to unroll all the leathern curtains. This rendered the interior of the wagon very dark and oppressively hot, there being no aperture for light or air excepting in front, between the driver and the passenger by his side. This obscurity and suffocation rendered more welcome the report of our driver at about three in the afternoon that we were approaching Georgetown. We entered this town in half an hour more, and descended from our prison at the " Fountain Tavern."

This day's journey had afforded nothing particularly interesting excepting the singularity of our travelling through the woods, and the appearance of a country just emerging from a state of nature. The luxuriance of the forests denoted a rich soil, but a very small part only of the country had as yet been cleared for cultivation. As population advanced the woods would of course disappear. In the meantime it was impossible to see man in this early stage of solitary seclusion without considering the difficulties and privations he endured while slowly preparing the comforts of civilized life for his posterity. In the whole course of the day I had not seen a blacksmith's nor a baker's shop; and as for *medical* assistance in case of sickness or accident amongst the scattered inhabitants, there apparently was none whatever in the country we had passed through.

I intended to proceed this afternoon to Mr. Law's house at Washington, distant only about five or six miles, but could not procure a conveyance of any kind. I therefore contented myself with walking about Georgetown. It is a small but neat town, situated on the left or northern bank of the Potomac, a few miles below what are called the lower falls of that river, there being other falls, particularly the Great and Seneca falls, higher up. These falls are, of course, a complete obstruction to the navigation; but societies formed by the inhabitants of Maryland, Baltimore, and Pennsylvania were about to form locks and canals for the purpose of avoiding these interruptions.

The Potomac is inconsiderable till it reaches the neighborhood of Georgetown, when it becomes a large river navigable to the sea, a distance of nearly three hundred miles, though, strictly speaking, it may perhaps be considered as terminating at its junction with the Chesapeak, about one hundred and fifty miles from the lower falls. The passage of the Potomac through the Blue Ridge is said to afford most beautiful scenery. Many of the geologists of the United States seem to think that the Blue Mountains were once the boundaries of an immense lake till the Susquehannah, Potomac, and other rivers burst through them.

In my walk about the town I saw several good houses, some in rows, others in a line, but detached, the intervals between them not being yet filled up. The road from Virginia and the Southern States, crossing the Potomac here, already gives an air of prosperity to this little town, and assures its future importance, whatever may be the fate of the projected metropolis. Georgetown must share its advantages, but be independent of its failure.

27th.—When the landlord of the "Fountain" found that I was going to Mr. Law's, he made every endeavor to procure me a carriage, but without success. He this morning, however, procured me a horse, and had him brought to the door soon after breakfast.

Leaving, therefore, my portmanteau to be forwarded in the course of the day, I set out for Washington, situated lower down the Potomac, in the territory of Columbia, the name given to a portion of land ceded by the contiguous States of Maryland and Virginia for the construction and convenience of the new metropolis.

Having crossed an extensive tract of level country somewhat resembling an English heath, I entered a large wood through which a very imperfect road had been made, principally by removing the trees, or rather the upper parts of them, in the usual manner. After some time this indistinct way assumed more the appearance of a regular avenue, the trees here having been cut down in a straight line. Although no habitation of any kind was visible, I had no doubt but I was now riding along one of the streets of the metropolitan city. I continued in this spacious avenue for half a mile, and then came out upon a large spot, cleared of wood, in the centre of which I saw two buildings on an extensive scale, and some men at work on one of them. The only human beings I should have seen here not a great many years before would have been some savages of the Potomac, whose tribe is said to have sent deputies to treat with William Penn at the assembly he held at Chester. Advancing and speaking to these workmen, they informed me that I was now in the centre of the city, and that the building before me was the Capitol, and the other destined to be a tavern. As the greatest cities have a similar beginning, there was really nothing surprising here, nor out of the usual order of things; but still the scene which surrounded me — the metropolis of a great nation in its first stage from a sylvan state — was strikingly singular. I thought it the more so, as the accounts which I had received of Washington while at Philadelphia, and the plan which I had seen hung up in the dining-room at Bladensburg, had prepared me for something rather more advanced. Looking from where I now stood I saw on every side a thick wood pierced with avenues in a more or less perfect state. These denoted the lines of the intended streets, which already appeared in the engraved plan with their future names. The Capitol promised to be a large and handsome building, judging from the part, about two thirds, already above the ground. I walked through several of the lower apartments, and saw the halls designed for the representatives and senate, now in an unfinished state, and encumbered with building materials. I did not go into the tavern. It was a large building of red brick, and in a much more advanced state than the Capitol, being roofed in.

The masons having answered all my questions with much civility, I rode on, following the avenue they pointed out to me. After going about three quarters of a mile through a silent wilderness, I found myself upon a trackless plain partially covered with trees and brushwood. I in vain looked about for Mr. Law's house or some one to guide me to it. I therefore rode on in the direction I judged the most likely to lead me out of this labyrinth. I knew that in case of my not succeeding, my retreat was always open to the Capitol, for while talking with the workmen I observed that all the avenues converged to that point. I continued therefore to explore my way through the thickets, keeping my horse's head rather towards the right, to gain, if necessary, the Potomac, whose bank I might then follow.

I had not proceeded far before I saw a carriage issue from the forest beyond the plain, and I soon perceived that it was making for a small bridge, which I now discovered for the first time, considerably to the right of the point for which I was making. I shaped my course accordingly, and hastened forward as fast as the nature of the ground would permit, that I might catch the carriage at the bridge, from which we were both at nearly the same distance. The carriage, however, was apparently trotting along upon a road, while my progress was almost stopped, and was soon likely to be quite so, by the bogginess of the land as I drew near a small stream that I found running along the bottom. Thus I saw the carriage pass the bridge, and escaping, while I was yet at some distance. It fortunately, however, turned afterwards rather to the right, making towards the wood I had left, and it seemed possible that I might still intercept it by regaining the high ground and getting to the road it was taking. I succeeded in this attempt, reaching the road just before it passed. As it approached the hope I had indulged was confirmed. It *was* Mr. Law's chariot, which, in the expectation of my arrival at Georgetown, Mr. Law had sent for me. The coachman tying my horse behind, we recrossed the small bridge, passed through the forest I had seen, and a second plain beyond it, and reached the banks of the Potomac. In a few minutes more we arrived at Mr. Law's, where I had a most cordial reception.

In the afternoon Mr. Law took me about his new estate. His house, built by himself, was only a few yards from the steep bank of the Potomac, and commanded a fine view across that river, here half a mile wide. In the rear of the house Mr. Law was building a street, consisting of much smaller houses than his own, speculating upon a great increase in their value when the expected transfer of the seat of government should be effected. The position at least was favorable, being on a point of land between the Potomac and a tributary stream called "the eastern branch," thus offering a double waterfront.

Mr. Law sent a servant to Georgetown with my horse, with directions to bring back my portmanteau.

In the evening Miss Westcott of Philadelphia arrived. Though possessing a sort of celebrity for her talents and literary attainments, her manners were particularly unaffected and agreeable.

28th.—Spent the day with Mr. Law's family. Monsieur Talleyrand, ex-bishop of Autun, whom the hostility of parties in France had driven across the Atlantic, was expected from Philadelphia, but much to my regret did not come.

29th.—Mr. and Mrs. Law took me in their carriage this forenoon to introduce me to Mr. Lear and his family, residing near Georgetown, but within the limits, as I understood, of the new city. The family was nearly related to General Washington. Mr. Lear himself was the General's private secretary. I thought him a most respectable man. The family inquired if I had been introduced to the President, and when they found that I had not, promised me a particular introduction on my return to Philadelphia.

Miss Custis, sister of Mrs. Law, arrived. A letter from Monsieur Talleyrand announced that he was under the necessity of deferring his visit. I had reckoned much upon the gratification of spending a few days thus privately in the company of this celebrated character. The talents and liveliness of Mr. Law, and the acquirements of Miss Westcott, were not ill calculated to produce some display of his powers, and elicit some sparks of his wit.

30th.—To-day Mr. and Mrs. Law were so good as to make a party on my account to Alexandria, which I had a desire to see, as one of the principal towns in Virginia. Accompanied by Miss Custis and Miss Westcott, we embarked in a large boat and were rowed down the Potomac. A little below the point on which Mr. Law's house stood, after the junction of the eastern branch, the river was nearly a mile in width, and remained without perceptible increase till we reached Alexandria, on the opposite or southern shore, seven miles lower. The current was rather slow than rapid. On both sides was a flat country, presenting no picturesque scenery towards the river. But a great river, seen for the first time, is itself an object of sufficient interest, and I accordingly felt great satisfaction in rowing down the Potomac, although the romantic scenes of which I had heard did not extend so low down its course.

Arrived at Alexandria, we landed at a handsome, recently built quay, nearly in the centre of the water-line, and walked up the town to the inn, passing in our way through a large open space, apparently intended for a market-place. The town, being built upon a slope from the interior to the water's edge, appeared to much advantage as we rowed towards it from the middle of the river. But the circumstance which most struck me was the vast number of houses which I saw building as we passed through the streets, and the number of people employed as carpenters and masons. The hammer and trowel were at work everywhere—a cheering sight, and a remarkable contrast with the dilapidation of cities which I had seen in my former travels. Although the latter were calculated to afford a deeper interest in some respects, the scene of new and active life, the foundations of future prosperity which Alexandria presented, made me feel how much more gratifying it is to observe the rise of a new state than the decline of an old one.

It appeared not improbable that Alexandria, situated lower down the Potomac, and enjoying the advantage of a greater depth of water, would in commercial competition prove a formidable rival to Washington. It is probable, however, that the immense back country, as it is called, of the United States will, when duly peopled, afford an ample commerce to all the great towns advantageously situated near the mouths of the principal rivers along the Atlantic coast.

I did not forget as I walked about the streets the assurance of the Virginians at Baltimore that I should probably see here persons who had lost an eye by gouging. Although I had not this demonstration, I was informed that the practice was by no means uncommon, and that there *were* persons in the town who had lost an eye in this manner.

After dining at the inn we returned to the boat. There not being wind enough to assist us against the stream, we got on but slowly with our oars. We lost nothing, however, by this delay but a little time, for the moon shone so beautifully upon the still, broad stream that we were all struck with the loveliness of the scene. Miss Westcott even made it the subject of some lines, whose elegance only I recollect.

1st May.— To-day having been fixed for my returning towards Philadelphia, there to embark for England, I received a very flattering letter of introduction to General Washington from his relations, whom I had visited with Mr. and Mrs. Law near Georgetown. They also intrusted me with a miniature picture of the general, which they wished me to deliver to him.

My stay with Mr. and Mrs. Law had been rendered extremely agreeable by the great kindness I had received from them. They wished me to prolong my stay, but I was anxious to get to England, particularly as I should be likely to sail again for India early in the following year.

Although Mr. Law seemed satisfied with his new situation, having a companion with whom a man might be happy anywhere, I could not but be surprised at the plan of life he had chosen. The clearing of ground and building of small houses, amongst the woods of the Potomac, seemed an uncongenial occupation for a man of so accomplished a mind, and whose former habits and employment had been so different. As chief of a large district in Bengal he had been accustomed to the discharge of important official functions, and to the splendor and consequence of a prince. In England his family was opulent and distinguished. One brother was bishop of Carlisle, another was a barrister of the first eminence, and the successful defender of Mr. Warren Hastings against the political influence of Fox, the eloquence of Sheridan, and the virulence of Burke. America, of all countries, seemed the least suited to the activity or leisure of such a person. Here almost every one was engaged either in politics or speculative enterprise. But as a foreigner, and particularly as an Englishman, Mr. Law could never possess any political weight in the country; and his inexperience in commercial affairs, amidst rivals so experienced and intelligent, might expose him to litigation and disappointment, and involve a considerable diminution of his fortune. One anticipation in which he indulged, with great confidence and satisfaction, was that *other* East-Indians would join him; and he hoped, I was sorry to see, that I might return to Bengal with impressions tending to encourage this migration. As we stood one evening on the bank of the river before his door, he said, "Here I will make a terrace, and we will sit and smoke our hookahs."

I deeply regretted this delusion. It seemed not improbable that East-Indians might sometimes take America in their way to England, as I had done; but I could not think, nor hardly hope, that they would desert the refined charms of the Thames, their families and country, to colonize and smoke their hookahs on the banks of the Potomac.

I left my kind friends, with the painful idea

that I should probably never see them again, soon after twelve o'clock. I was unwilling to take their carriage and horses farther than Georgetown, through which the stage-wagon from Virginia would pass the next morning; but they insisted upon my going in it as far as Bladensburg. As Miss Westcott was going to Georgetown, I had the pleasure of her company so far. She stopped at the house of Mr. Stuart, where she introduced me to her friends the Misses Breck, two other young ladies from Philadelphia. Having remained here a short time, I continued my ride to Bladensburg, and, alighting there at the "Indian Queen," was well taken care of the rest of the afternoon by Mr. Ross. I observed that Mr. Law's coachman was well provided against the deficiencies of the country, having spare shoes for his horses and the necessary instruments of a blacksmith's shop.

2d May.—The stage-wagon arriving soon after breakfast, I take leave of Mr. Ross. Changed horses at Van's, and again at Spurrier's, where we dined. The day being very fine and my five or six companions very agreeable men, I enjoyed my ride, amused with the rude beginnings of civilization which I again saw on every side, and contemplating the changes which human energy and perseverance would gradually introduce. From the summit of a hill leading down to the Patapsco, I enjoyed the only fine view upon the road, though the partial clearing of the woods would undoubtedly discover, and form indeed, others. At four o'clock we drove into the great yard of the "Indian Queen," when the landlord jocosely expressed his satisfaction at seeing me return with both my eyes from Virginia.

Having noticed some unusual bustle about the streets, I was informed that there had been a review of the militia that morning to celebrate the anniversary of St. Tammany, the titular saint of America. St. Tammany's Day was the day before, but that being Sunday, the celebration of it had been deferred till to-day. In the evening I went to the play. It was performed by French comedians, the greater part of whom were unfortunate persons whom the tyranny of the Revolution had driven from their country and from better situations in life.

3d.—Unwell to-day, with a slight return of my Indian symptoms. I, however, paid visits to the friends who had before shown me so much kindness. I received several invitations to dinner, but preferred dining alone at the inn. In the afternoon I took a very pleasant ride on horseback, accompanied by the two young Messrs. Gilmore. They took me round the port to some high ground commanding a good view of the town, the basin, and shipping. I spent the evening very agreeably with the Misses Stith. I regret that my journal does not mention, and that I cannot recollect, who these ladies were, nor how I was introduced to them. They had the goodness to procure me some English newspapers I was desirous of seeing. I had been told in Philadelphia that my sister had been married to a surgeon, and I thought the newspapers might give me more particulars. On my return home, I found that Mr. Field, the miniature painter, had called.

4th.—Called upon Mr. Field and *sat*. Dined with a large party at Mr. Campbell's, the President of the St. George's Society.

5th.—Sat again to Mr. Field. Mr. Consul Barry called, and afterwards Colonels Howard and O'Donald, two of the principal inhabitants of Baltimore. They both gave most friendly invitations to their country-seats—the former to Belvidere, of which I had heard much, and Colonel O'Donald to his villa, called Canton. Colonel O'Donald had, many years before, been in Bengal, and now expressed much pleasure in meeting one from that country. Called upon Mr. Thornton; further conversation with him about Pembroke Hall. Called upon Mr. Curzon. Singular particulars of his family.* He informed me that Mr. Robert Liston had arrived in Philadelphia, as British Plenipotentiary to the United States. I afterwards saw the Danish Consul. He informed me that he had received a letter from Dr. Ross, of Philadelphia, in which he was pleased to speak of me in very friendly terms, and to approve of my opinions respecting America. Mr. Barry read part of the doctor's letter. He mentioned having introduced me to Dr. Priestley, and the doctor's satisfaction with some communications about India. He said that Dr. Priestley meant to make an acknowledgment in a book he was about to publish.

6th.—As I was walking up and down the great room before breakfast this morning,

---

* My journal does not state these particulars, and I have entirely forgotten them.

Mr. Volney came up to me. He had arrived from Philadelphia the evening before. He confirmed the news of Mr. Liston's appointment and arrival.

Colonel O'Donald called to invite me to meet a party of his friends at Canton on the following Sunday. Dined with Mr. Consul Barry off salt fish, it being Friday.

7th.—I walked this morning to breakfast with Colonel Howard at Belvidere, only about half a mile from the top of the town to the right. The beauty of this seat exceeded even the accounts which I had received of it. It was upon the plan and possessed all the elegance of an English villa. Situated upon the verge of the descent upon which Baltimore stands, its grounds formed a beautiful slant towards the Chesapeak. From the taste with which they were laid out, it would seem that America already possessed a Haverfield or a Repton. The spot, thus indebted to nature and judiciously embellished, was as enchanting within its own proper limits as in the fine view which extended far beyond them. The foreground presented luxurious shrubberies and sloping lawns: the distance, the line of the Patapsco, and the country bordering on Chesapeak Bay. *Both* the perfections of the landscape, its near and distant scenery, were united in the view from the bow-window of the noble room in which breakfast was prepared, with the desire, I believe, of gratifying me with this exquisite prospect. I could not help thinking that if Mr. Law or other nabobs chose to abandon their own country for America, *such* was the residence they should look for. I spent the greater part of the forenoon at Belvidere, detained by the attentions of Colonel Howard's family and the attractions of his villa, which seemed hardly to belong to the same age or country as the forests I had just passed through in so rude a conveyance; and it was indeed, less a specimen of the actual state of general improvement than evidence of the refinement towards which society in America was advancing.

I had intended to walk back to Baltimore, but Colonel Howard would order his carriage for me. I was accompanied by two young ladies of the name of Chew, who were staying at Belvidere, and took this opportunity of *shopping* and paying a few visits.

I dined with Mr. Gilmore's family, and stayed till a late hour.

8th.—Called upon Mr. Campbell and Mr.

Thomson. Early in the afternoon the friends of Colonel O'Donald who were to dine with him called upon me at his desire to accompany me to his country-house—distant about seven miles. Having mounted my horse, we proceeded down Market Street, and when nearly at the bottom of the town turned to the left and gained the country extending along the basin of the Patapsco. The road being rough and stony, my companions supposed I should wish to go slowly, but knowing the taste of the Americans for fast riding, I took the lead at a quick pace. We reached Canton after a merry ride. I was led to think from what I saw now, and had before observed, that the Americans have more spirits and vivacity on such occasions than the English, or, at least, that their impressions are under less reserve. It is to this unreserved communication probably that the facility with which the Americans express themselves in conversation is to be attributed. An American speaks English with the volubility of a Frenchman. On my arrival in America I was much struck with this peculiarity. The day before I embarked at Calcutta I called upon Sir Robert Abercromby to take leave of him, to thank him for the numerous acts of kindness I had received from him, and to see him, *in fact*, though I then little thought of such being the case, for the last time. We walked up and down his great drawing-room from one end of it to the other for nearly, I believe, an hour; and speaking during part of this time of America, he told me of many things I should find there; but I do not recollect that this colloquial facility mentioned above was one of the number. If I had visited the veteran general in his retirement on the banks of the Forth (and deep is my regret that I did not), how many things I should have had to say to him about America as well as India!

Colonel O'Donald had shown his Indian predilection in the construction of his residence as well as in its name. The long, low house, with a deep veranda in front, had somewhat the appearance of a pucka bungalow. It was pleasantly situated amongst fields and small woods, not far from the junction of the Patapsco with the Chesapeak. The Colonel told me that when he was in Calcutta he had a great desire to visit the interior of India, and particularly Lucnow. My journey into the same part of the country seemed to afford him considerable interest, as did my imperial seal. He appeared to wish that he had passed more years in India and fewer in America. Nothing was omitted to testify his satisfaction at seeing me, and I should gladly have accepted his invitation to pass two or three days at Canton if time had permitted me. After a sumptuous dinner the Colonel's friends accompanied me back to Baltimore, and even to the door of my hotel. This was one of the most pleasant days I passed in America.

Though late, I went, agreeably to an engagement I had made previously, to take a second cup of tea with Mr. Field, and sat with him till one o'clock in the morning. I do not know what became of his picture.

9th.—At dinner to-day I sat next to Monsieur Volney and had much conversation with him about India, respecting which country he was always very inquisitive. He asked me what precautions I had adopted in my journeys there, and whether I had disguised myself. I said that as I could speak the language of the people disguise would have been easy and perhaps the safest expedient, but that I felt there was something degrading in this resource, and never adopted it except on one occasion of sudden emergency. I had also, I said, departed from the custom of some travellers in another respect. Instead of passing for a person of no consequence, I assumed all the importance I was entitled to, and sometimes indeed rather more. This put me in relation with the chiefs of the country, and the heads of towns and villages, and placed my party in some measure under the responsibility and protection of the official authorities. Instead of entering a town as a person desiring concealment, I announced my arrival by the most intelligent and best-dressed of my suite, and asked for everything that a stranger of consideration had a right to expect. As far as my means would allow I travelled with a force calculated to command respect on common occasions as an escort, and capable of making a good defence in case of attack. When I thought that my guard was not proportioned to some particular danger we were likely to encounter, I sent to the aumil, or governor, of the country, or to the chief of the place, and, stating who I was, asked for such an increase of force as he himself judged necessary; and on these occasions I never met with a refusal. I added that though I did not adopt disguise in the usual sense of the word, I so far assumed the national dress as not to shock the prejudices of the people or excite an inconvenient degree of curiosity; but that, so far from adopting this step as a deception, I always left enough of my proper character to show the inhabitants that my object was to conciliate and not to mislead them. Monsieur Volney expressed his concurrence with these plans, and said he would adopt them if he should ever gratify his desire of visiting India, as he believed he might but for the length of the sea voyage. He described what he suffered on coming from France to America, and said he could not think of another voyage without horror.

After dinner Monsieur Volney and I walked out together. He told me he should probably publish some account of America. He examined things as we went about very minutely, and in some of his surveys made me his assistant. Having taken the measure of my step, he requested me to walk from one side of the street to the other, while he with his pocket-book in his hand counted the number of my paces, and noted down their equivalent in feet. We went also into one of the principal churches. But though I was gratified with this unexpected intercourse with so distinguished a man, I cannot say that Monsieur Volney pleased me much. He was cold and satirical. I did not perceive that he had any communication with any one at Baltimore but myself. I concluded that the political troubles in which he had been engaged, and the persecution which had banished him from his country, had caused this splenetic unsociableness or increased a constitutional irritability. He was little pleased with America, and where he was not pleased he expressed himself with much severity. As a philosopher he might be expected to see with less surprise and dissatisfaction the imperfections of a new state, so remote from the improvements and influence of Europe; and as the guest of America he might be expected to repay her hospitality with more urbanity and indulgence.

In the evening I met with surprise Mr. Pringle, the supercargo of the *India*. I received a visit from Mr. Grove, merchant, of Baltimore, and connected, I understood, with Mr. Gilmore's house. Mr. Gilmore wished me to make some communications to him respecting the commerce of India.

Although Baltimore is the principal town of Maryland as to population and commerce,

Annapolis, about thirty miles distant, is the seat of the provincial government. The population of the town was said not to exceed 20,000; that of the state was about 350,000, of which nearly the third part were slaves, employed principally in the cultivation of tobacco and wheat, the staple commodities of the export trade. Baltimore was founded by Lord Baltimore in the reign of Charles the First.

10th May.—At 6 A.M. I set out for Philadelphia. Among the passengers who almost filled the wagon was Mr. Hancock, son of Mr. Hancock of Massachusetts, the countryman and colleague of Mr. Adams, the Vice-President. A trifling circumstance showed the general feeling of respect towards General Washington. Mr. Hancock having learned that I was bearer of the picture of the General, communicated this incident to the rest of the company, upon whom it seemed to make an extraordinary impression, procuring me their congratulations on being honored with such a charge, and particular marks of their attention during the remainder of the journey.

Breakfasted at Harford. Stopped a few minutes at Charlestown, from the neighborhood of which is a fine view of the Chesapeak. Dined at Havre de Grace. The dinner, though not remarkable for its excellence, afforded by its singularity much amusement. The first dish being pork, to which one of the passengers, a Frenchman, had a great dislike, he waited for the second, but this being pork also his national irritability was much excited, and broke through all bounds when he found that the remaining dishes were only varieties of the same hated food. The Frenchman, who had perhaps calculated on a fine trout from the Susquehannah, expressed his dissatisfaction in very warm terms; and when finally a rather high bill was placed before us, he positively refused his share of the contribution. The American *in*sisted, the Frenchman *re*sisted, and seconded his declaration by twice raising his knife and striking the handle of it with great violence against the table. It would have been fortunate if his resentment had ended here, for lifting up his knife a third time, while he looked angrily at the master of the inn, he brought the end of it down, not upon the table, but on his plate and broke it to pieces. The landlord was far from disposed to soothe the increased vexation of his offended guest, but said with an air of triumph, "Monsieur will now pay for the dinner and the plate too"; and in fact, instead of reducing his bill or the Frenchman's portion, he charged as liberally for his porcelain as for his pork; leaving the Frenchman no other satisfaction than that of complaining during the rest of the journey that he had paid dear for a dinner he had not eaten, and for more plates than he had broken. For myself I not only made a good dinner, the pork being excellent, but learned a circumstance which itself was worth my share of the reckoning. I was informed that great numbers of pigs were turned loose into the woods of the Susquehannah, where they run wild, living and growing fat upon the acorns and nuts of various sorts which abound there. Before winter the poor animals are hunted, and such as are caught—for many probably escape—are killed for home consumption and exportation. I was told that a similar plan was adopted in other parts of Maryland, and it most likely extended to other states.

I had heard on board the *India*, and indeed Sir Robert Abercromby had before mentioned the circumstance to me, that in some parts of America the pigs were fed on peaches. I now found that this was the fact, and not so extraordinary a one as it had at first seemed to be. I had observed to-day, as I had in other parts of Maryland, that almost every farm-house and cottage had a peach orchard attached to it, as an apple orchard would be in England. The peaches were distilled into brandy, but the pigs fed upon the refuse, as well as upon such fruit as fell from the trees.

As we crossed the Susquehannah, I cast a farewell look upon the wild beauties of that river. It was dark before we reached the "Head of Elk." Here things were much changed since I passed before. There was indeed the same number of beds in the room, but the landlord was no longer surly, but extremely civil, and gave us a supper that made the best possible amends to the Frenchman for the loss of his dinner.

11th May.—Leave the "Head of Elk" at five o'clock. Breakfast at Newark, and at three in the afternoon reach Philadelphia. Finding dinner prepared at the inn, I dined there and afterwards proceeded to Fourth Street, where Mr. and Mrs. Francis, and the good-tempered negress, and all my friends, were glad to see me. My notes say, "Glad to get to a good mattress again." In the evening I went to the play, the " Moghol Tale."

The excursion which I had made had quite succeeded. The country, towns, villages, state of society, were full of interest in their present condition, while their futurity presented a picture the most pleasing—the forests I had passed through converted into fertile plains, and the solitary banks of the Potomac, the Susquehannah, the Elk, and the Patapsco, covered with a free and intelligent population. One of the many improvements already spoken of is the junction of the Chesapeak and Delaware by cutting through the isthmus which now separates them. There will then be an inland water communication between Philadelphia, Annapolis, Alexandria, and Washington.

12th May.—Hearing that the American ship *Atlantic* would sail in a few days for England, I walked down to the Delaware, and liking the appearance of the vessel, I took my passage in her, engaging one of the state-rooms, a name rather absurdly bestowed upon a very small berth by the side of the great cabin or public-room, and feebly lighted from it by a glass in the door. The ship appeared to be about 300 tons, or nearly the size of the *India*. Called afterwards at Mr. Bingham's, where I found my Cabul sheep grazing in good health on the garden lawn. Visited Dr. Ross and other friends.

13th May.—At one o'clock to-day I called at General Washington's with the picture and letter I had for him. He lived in a small red brick house on the left side of High Street, not much higher up than Fourth Street. There was nothing in the exterior of the house that denoted the rank of its possessor. Next door was a hair-dresser. Having stated my object to a servant who came to the door, I was conducted up a neat but rather narrow staircase, carpeted in the middle, and was shown into a middling-sized, well-furnished drawing-room on the left of the passage. Nearly opposite the door was the fireplace, with a wood-fire in it. The floor was carpeted. On the left of the fireplace was a sofa, which sloped across the room. There were no pictures on the walls, no ornaments on the chimney-piece. Two windows on the right of the entrance looked into the street. There was nobody in the room, but in a minute Mrs. Washington came in, when I repeated the object of my calling, and put into her hands the letter for General Washington, and his miniature. She said she would deliver them to the President, and, inviting me to sit down, retired for that purpose. She soon returned, and said the President would come presently. Mrs. Washington was a middle-sized lady, rather stout; her manner extremely kind and unaffected. She sat down on the sofa, and invited me to sit by her. I spoke of the pleasant days I had passed at Washington, and of the attentions I had received from her granddaughter, Mrs. Law.

While engaged in this conversation, but with my thoughts turned to the expected arrival of the General, the door opened, and Mrs. Washington and myself rising, she said, "The President," and introduced me to him. Never did I feel more interest than at this moment, when I saw the tall, upright, venerable figure of this great man advancing towards me to take me by the hand. There was a seriousness in his manner which seemed to contribute to the impressive dignity of his person, without diminishing the confidence and ease which the benevolence of his countenance and the kindness of his address inspired. There are persons in whose appearance one looks in vain for the qualities they are known to possess, but the appearance of General Washington harmonized in a singular manner with the dignity and modesty of his public life. So completely did he *look* the great and good man he really was, that I felt rather respect than awe in his presence, and experienced neither the surprise nor disappointment with which a personal introduction to distinguished individuals is often accompanied.

The General having thanked me for the picture, requested me to sit down next the fire, Mrs. Washington being on the sofa on the other side, and himself taking a chair in the middle. He now inquired about my arrival in America, my voyage, my late journey, and his granddaughters, Mrs. Law and her sister, who had accompanied me to Alexandria. He asked me my opinion of that town, and seemed pleased with the account I gave of the extraordinary activity I had observed there. In the course of the conversation I mentioned the particular regard and respect with which Lord Cornwallis always spoke of him. He received this communication in the most courteous manner, inquired about his lordship, and expressed for him much esteem.

Speaking about the intercourse between India and America, I said that I thought the United States had gained a great point by the right of trading conceded by the thirteenth article of Mr. Jay's treaty, and I mentioned at the same time the facilities of which this commerce was susceptible, to the equal advantage of America and India, now that it rested upon a legal basis.

I stated these opinions because the treaty in question, which had been approved by the existing Government, had caused some unreasonable animadversion amongst the opposers of the administration at this period. I observed that the measure was one to which the East India Company might object, as interfering with their chartered privileges, although in a manner favorable to the commercial population of India; but that it was in every respect advantageous to the United States, enlarging a communication that before was confined, and legalizing what was arbitrary and subject to prohibition.

The General asked me some questions about Calcutta, the natives of India, the Ganges, and the interior of the country. Upon my inquiring if coal had yet been found in the States of the Union, he said that it had been discovered in various parts, and that mines would doubtless be opened and worked when the diminished abundance of wood should direct the public attention to this subject.

After sitting about three quarters of an hour, I rose to take leave, when the General invited me to drink tea with him that evening. I regret to say that I declined this honor on account of some other engagement—a wrong and injudicious decision, for which I have since reproached myself. No engagement should have prevented my accepting such an invitation. If forwardness on such occasions be displeasing, an excess of delicacy and reserve is scarcely less to be avoided. However, this private intercourse with one of the most unblemished characters that any country has produced had entirely satisfied me, and greatly exceeded my previous expectations, which had been limited to the usual transient introduction at a public levee. This, then, forms one of my most memorable days. The moment when the great Washington entered the room, and Mrs. Washington said, "The President," made an impression on my mind which no subsequent years can efface.

The General's age was rather more than

sixty-four. In person he was tall, well-proportioned, and upright. His hair was powdered and tied behind. Although his deportment was that of a general, the expression of his features had rather the calm dignity of a legislator than the severity of a soldier. He was born in Virginia, and was now contemplating his final retirement to Mount Vernon, his favorite residence, situated in that State, a few miles only below Alexandria. Shortly after the period of my introduction he expressed his intentions in a feeling address, of which the following are a few extracts:

"Friends and Fellow-Citizens,—The period for a new election of a citizen to administer the Executive Government of the United States being not far distant, and the time being actually arrived when your thoughts must be employed in designating the person who is to be clothed with that important trust, it appears to me proper to conduce to a more distinct expression of the public voice, that I should now apprise you of the resolution I have formed, to decline being considered among the number of those of whom a choice is to be made. I confidently hoped it would have been much earlier in my power, consistently with motives which I am not at liberty to disregard, to return to that retirement from which I had been reluctantly drawn. Every day the increasing weight of years admonishes me more and more that the shade of retirement is as necessary as it is welcome. Satisfied that, if any circumstances have given peculiar value to my services, they were temporary, I have the consolation to believe that while choice and prudence invite me to quit the political scene, patriotism does not forbid me.

"In looking forward to the moment which is intended to terminate the career of my public life, my feelings do not permit me to suspend the deep acknowledgment of that debt of gratitude which I owe to my beloved country, for the many honors it has conferred upon me. The constancy of your support was the essential prop of my efforts, and the guarantee of my plans. Profoundly penetrated with this idea, I shall carry it with me to the grave, as a strong incitement to unceasing vows, that Heaven may continue to you the choicest tokens of its beneficence; that your union and brotherly love may be perpetual; that the free Constitution which is the work of your hands may be sacredly maintained; that its administration in every part may be stamped with wisdom and virtue; that, in fine, the happiness of the people of these States, under the auspices of liberty, may be made complete by so careful a preservation and so prudent a use of this blessing, as will acquire to them the glory of recommending it to the applause, the affection, and adoption of every nation which is a stranger to it.

"Observe good faith and justice towards all nations; cultivate peace and harmony with all. How far, in the discharge of my official duties, I have been governed by the principles which I have delineated, the public records, and other evidences of my conduct, must witness to you and to the world. To myself, the assurance of my own conscience is, that I have, at least, believed myself to be guided by them. Though, in reviewing the incidents of my administration, I am unconscious of intentional error, I am nevertheless too sensible of my defects not to think it probable I have committed many errors. Whatever they may be, I fervently beseech the Almighty to avert or mitigate the evils to which they may tend. I shall also carry with me the hope that my country will never cease to view them with indulgence, and that after forty-five years of my life dedicated to its service, with an upright zeal, the faults of incompetent abilities will be consigned to oblivion, as myself must soon be to the mansions of rest. Relying on its kindness in this and other things, and actuated by that fervent love towards it which is natural to a man who views in it the native soil of himself and family for several generations, I anticipate, with pleasing expectation, that retreat in which I promise myself to realize, without alloy, the sweet enjoyment of partaking, in the midst of my fellow-citizens, of the benign influence of good laws under a free Government, the everfavorite object of my heart, and the happy reward, as I trust, of our cares, labors, and dangers."

General Washington had retired to Mount Vernon at the close of the war, and remained there till 1789, when the general voice of his country called him from his pastoral pursuits to the Presidency of the Government. He was re-elected to this office in 1793. His healthy and robust appearance, when I saw him, seemed to promise a longer enjoyment of repose in his retirement near the banks of the Potomac; but a cold caught at Mount Vernon on the 13th December, 1799, terminated his life on the following day.

14th. — Visited the National Museum. Amongst a collection of curiosities, yet in its commencement, I saw my great shell.

15th. — Being unwell, I spent the greater part of this day at home. Packed and prepared for my voyage.

Sunday, 16th. — In a sermon Dr. Priestley preached to-day, he referred to what I had said to him about the Hindoos. Dined with Mr. Bingham, Mr. Baring, Count de Noailles, and several members of the two Houses of Congress — in all a large party. After the company had retired, remained with the family* and Mr. Baring.

17th.—Saw Captain Langford, and found that his ship, the *Atlantic*, would not sail for some days. In consequence of this delay, I determined to set out for New York, to endeavor to find out a friend there, about whom I could obtain no information. We had been intimate at school before I sailed for India; and though our wide separation—he in the New World, I in the Old—had put an end to all communication, it had not diminished my regard for him. I took my place in the New York stage-wagon for the next day.

18th.—At 5 P.M. start for New York with other passengers. The carriage was exactly similar to those already described. The first stage was through Frankfort, Holmsburgh, and Harlington, inconsiderable villages nearly at equal distances from each other, to Bristol, twelve miles from Philadelphia. The Delaware was only a short distance from us, on our right, but was not visible. Its course here was about southwest, and our direction was nearly parallel to it, or northeast. Hav-

---

* The family consisted of Mr. and Mrs. Bingham and two daughters, the eldest of whom was afterwards married to the Mr. Baring here mentioned, afterwards Lord Ashburton.

ing changed horses at Bristol, we passed through the hamlets of Tullytown and Tyburn to Morrisville, or Morristown, as it is also called, and soon after arrived on the banks of the Delaware, here considerably less wide than at Philadelphia. A large flat-bottomed boat took us over to Trenton, a small town, but the metropolis of the State of New Jersey, which we entered here. This is the highest point to which the Delaware is navigable, there being falls above the ferry, similar to those on the Potomac above Georgetown, and both apparently proceeding from the same cause, the depression or lower level of the country east of the Blue Ridge.

Trenton was the scene of a brilliant exploit of General Washington during the late war. A regiment of Hessians, in the pay of Great Britain, being stationed there, Washington formed a plan for surprising it. Having thrown some troops across the river, just below the falls, to get into the rear of the enemy and cut off their retreat, he fixed upon the night of Christmas Day for passing the river himself at the ferry, and notwithstanding the greatest obstacles, arising from the darkness and from the difficulty of the passage, obstructed by ice, succeeded in surprising the detachment so completely that he took nine hundred men and several pieces of artillery.

19th.—At Trenton we left the Delaware and proceeded in a northeasterly direction across New Jersey. Early in the morning we reached Princeton, another place, like Trenton and Brandywine, grateful to the recollection of the Americans; General Washington having in the year 1777, not long after his success against the Hessians, surprised and dislodged a considerable British force stationed here. Princeton possesses one of the largest colleges in the United States. Its situation between two of the principal cities of the Union appears favorable to such an institution, particularly as the position is pleasant and salubrious. It is a large stone building, not far from the road-side. I walked towards it while the wagon stopped, but had not time to see the interior. Its library was said to exceed three thousand volumes.

At the distance of eight miles from Princeton we reached Brunswick, situated on the banks of the Raritan River, about twelve miles from its entrance into Raritan Bay at Perth Amboy. Here also is a college called Queen's College. Small sea craft passing through Raritan Bay can come nearly as high as the handsome bridge which has lately been built at this town. We next passed through Elizabethtown, pleasantly situated upon a small stream of which I did not learn the name. It doubtless flowed from the line of hills in the interior, and ran into Raritan Bay.

Seven miles farther we came to Newark, which I thought one of the neatest and prettiest towns I had seen. I was told that many families of Dutch extraction resided here, and it appeared that they kept up their national habits of order and cleanliness. I was struck with the pleasant situation of some white detached houses which I observed on some high ground a few hundred yards to the left of the road. I told my companions that if I settled in America I should be induced to prefer that spot to any I had yet seen.

Soon after leaving Newark we came to the edge of a steep hill leading down to a long wooden bridge over the Passaic. The wagon being full, the driver stopped, and begged a negro, who was sitting by his side, to walk down the hill; and but for the inconvenience of getting out of the wagon, he would probably have desired the other passengers to do the same. The inability of the horses to keep back the carriage was soon apparent, and became more manifest every moment. They twice, however, succeeded in checking it for an instant, but were overpowered by the weight, and forced forward with greater violence than before, and were so little under command that it seemed not improbable, even if we got to the bottom of the descent, that we should either run against the bridge or go into the river, to which there was a wide opening on each side. Again, however, the wheelers, throwing themselves back, stopped the wagon, but the leaders, for some reason or other, got round with their heads towards the hill. In this state of disorder it was difficult to foresee what would be the effect of the next plunge. It was evident, at all events, that this was the moment for escaping from the carriage. This idea seemed to strike all the passengers at once, for all were in motion scrambling to get out. To such as were upon the front and hindmost benches there was no great difficulty, but they who, like myself, were upon the middle seat could not stir till the others made way; and there was no time to lose. Finding, therefore, that I could not get out either behind or before, I mounted upon the side rail and jumped, or rather dropped down, for I was so doubled by the roof and so kept back by the great leather curtain that it was quite impossible to make a proper spring; and I consequently fell perpendicularly down before the off hind wheel, and reaching the ground in a bent position I rolled under the wagon, or, rather, partly under it, so that the wheel must have passed over me if one of the passengers, who had escaped from behind, had not run and drawn me clear. The leaders having been pulled straight, the wheelers again threw themselves forward, and before I was upon my legs all four went off at full gallop, my companions in the middle seat still in their places, not having had time to escape. It was painful to see the danger to which these persons and the coachman were exposed, for it seemed very doubtful whether the latter would be able to hit the bridge, which was much narrower than the opening on either side leading to the water. But we soon had the satisfaction of seeing the stage safe upon the planks, along which it went at a great rate, the driver not being able to stop the horses. The negro, who had now reached the middle of the bridge, hearing the carriage come clattering behind him, got out of the way, not however to insure his own safety, but to risk his life in a daring attempt to save the persons still in the wagon. He held himself close to the side of the bridge ready to make a dash, and when the leaders came opposite to him, sprang forward and seized the bridle of the near horse. All, however, still continued to gallop, dragging the negro with them; but this bold African kept his hold, and the driver pulling at the same time, they were stopped a short distance beyond the bridge.

My attention had been so engaged with this singular spectacle that I had scarcely thought of a cut I had received on my right leg. I could not very well tell how this happened, whether by a stone in the road or by my having grazed against the hind wheel as I fell. One of the passengers kindly lending me his arm, I crossed the bridge and resumed my place in the wagon. My leg becoming very painful, the passengers seated before me obligingly made room for me to rest it on their bench, and were in every respect most polite and civil. Four miles farther we came to a bridge over the Hackinsack, a small river that runs into Newark Bay. Two miles farther the country became low and wet, having the appearance of a great swamp formed by the inundations of the Hudson, which we were now approaching, or by the encroachment of the waters of Raritan Bay, which may be considered the Chesapeak of the Jersey States. The road across this marsh was formed by trees laid across it and covered with earth. Though we went slowly here, the jolting as the wheels passed from tree to tree was very great, and caused much uneasiness to my leg, which had swelled considerably.

After a mile and a half of this most rough road we arrived at Pawles Hook, situated on the edge of New York Bay, and immediately opposite that city. Though yet but a small village, it reminded my companions of an event honorable to the arms of their country, a British post having been surprised here during the war by Major Lee, one of the most distinguished officers of the American army. Here we embarked in a large boat, and the wind being favorable, had a fine sail across the bay, whose width exceeded two miles. The view of New York in front, of the more expanded bay and three small islands to the right, and the Hudson on our left, was magnificent. I could neither conceal nor express the surprise and delight it afforded me.

Having landed at a quay in the eastern part of the city, we proceeded through several narrow streets to the inn. The state of my leg would have induced me to remain here, but the situation was not desirable, and a noted boarding-house at the end of Broadway had been particularly recommended to me. The same friendly Samaritan from whom I had already received so much attention became my guide to it, but on our way he prevailed on me to accompany him first to a surgeon, a friend of his. In a country where a gentleman's coachman is obliged to be his own smith, it was not surprising that a surgeon should be an apothecary, as no beggarly account of empty *bottles* showed this practitioner to be. I had much difficulty in persuading my kind companion to leave me in the hands in which he had placed me, nor would he consent to this till his friend had ascertained that my leg was not materially injured, though the necessity, he announced whilst dressing it, of a few days' rest was particularly unwelcome, on account of the sailing of the *Atlantic*, in which I had taken my passage, as well as of the mortification of being confined to my room during my stay in New York.

I easily found my way to the great boarding-house, but the first thing I learned here was that every room was engaged. This was a great disappointment to me, both on account of my lameness and the singular advantage of the situation, the house being close to the Battery, which had formed so fine an object in our passage across the river, and from which there is a view which has not, perhaps, many rivals in the world, commanding the bay of New York, four miles wide, and its three islands, the Hudson, the Jersey shore, the opening into Newark Bay, and the whole length of the river to Fort La Fayette on the northern, and Sandy Hook on the southern shore of the entrance into the Atlantic. All this, enlivened by the great passage to Pawles Hook, on the Jersey shore, and the numberless sails employed in the great maritime and inland commerce of New York, presented a splendid scene, and made me regret that I could not be admitted into Mrs. Hodge's boarding-house, the " Star and Garter" of this fine prospect. I accordingly hobbled back up Broadway, and then turned to the right, nearly in the direction of the quay at which I had landed, inquiring as I went for a good tavern, but could not hear of one. Everybody recommended me to Mrs. Hodge's, the house I had just left.

It being now almost dark, and my leg becoming more inflamed and painful, I allowed a civil man, to whom I applied in the street, to conduct me to a small boarding-house not far from the City Hall, which we passed. The kind behavior of the ladies who received me, the real concern they expressed at the state in which I presented myself, satisfied me that the dull little room which they showed me was, as they declared, the best they had, and induced me to accept it thankfully. These good women soon had tea ready for me in their parlor, and their attentions at once banished all regret that the window of my chamber did not look upon the fine view from the Battery. They expressed some surprise when they found that I came from India. I hoped to obtain some information from them about Mr. Shaw, but they were not acquainted with him.

20th.—After breakfasting with the ladies of the house, I walked to my surgeon, who still urged rest, the most inconvenient remedy in my present position. Neither could he give me any information about my schoolfellow. But I recollected hearing the latter speak of his uncle, Mr. John Shaw, and having obtained *his* address, I went to his house. He received me in the American way, with his hat on, at the top of his steps, and without any invitation to walk in. He evinced but little interest in my inquiries, and seemed to know but little about his nephew; but he told me where I might hear of him, and with this information I set off. I judged from this interview that the uncle and nephew were not upon the best terms—a notion, indeed, with which I had been somewhat impressed before.

I found out the small street and small house to which I had been directed, but was told by the maid who opened the door that Mr. Gabriel Shaw was not in New York. Two ladies of the house to whom I desired the maid to introduce me, confirmed this unexpected intelligence, with the kindest expression of sympathy in my disappointment. They said he was absent with some friends on a foot excursion, and that the time of his return was uncertain. I left my address, and promised to return the next morning. I spent the rest of the day at my lodging, principally in the agreeable society of the ladies of the house. I was the only lodger, but two or three gentlemen came to dinner.

21st.—Called at Mr. Shaw's lodging, but the ladies could only repeat what they had told me the preceding day. Mr. Shaw's return being thus uncertain, I should have set out for Philadelphia immediately if my lameness had permitted me to travel, for I was much afraid of losing my passage in the *Atlantic*. I remained at home till the afternoon, and then walked with my stick to the quays situated upon the entrance into East River, a narrow channel which separates Long Island from the continent. I saw many vessels, principally American, alongside the wharfs, to which there is a direct and safe access from the sea, through the fine bay, called the Bay of New York, formed by the Hudson in the lower part of its course, a spacious navigation of only twenty miles from the Narrows, or entrance from the Atlantic Ocean. With these advantages, New York, for maritime communication, possesses an evident superiority over Philadelphia, Baltimore, Alexandria, and Washington, and may consequently be considered the first port of the United States. It possesses other advantages not less evident, in an extraordinary facility of intercourse with an extensive and already populous interior, by means of the Hudson River, navigable for small sloops for nearly 200 miles from the sea, thus affording a communication with Albany, 150 miles above New York, and thence with the whole country bordering upon Lakes Erie, Ontario, and Michigan, the first 230 miles in length, the second 180, and the last, which is entirely American, 300.

Albany, situated on the west bank of the Hudson, half-way between these lakes and New York, can hardly fail of acquiring great commercial importance, as the vast countries which encircle these inland seas shall advance in population and prosperity. I heard an intelligent American — and few are the Americans who are not intelligent upon every subject requiring judgment and foresight — declare that if he were to buy land anywhere, he would prefer Albany to any spot in the Union. The only circumstance unfavorable to this position that I heard of was the impetuosity of the Hudson, which rendered its navigation slow and expensive, and somewhat dangerous. It was observed, however, that this same rapidity of the current prevented the accumulation of ice, by which most of the American rivers are obstructed for a considerable time during the winter.

From the quays in Water Street, along the shores of the East River, I rounded the point till I came to the Battery at the end of Broadway, and from the handsome promenade which has been made here I contemplated with more leisure than the first evening the admirable view this spot commands. I recalled to my recollection the principal cities I had seen, and could find no one in this review whose situation was at once so advantageous and beautiful as that of New York. The only defect I could perceive was its apparent exposure in time of war. An enemy's squadron could in the present state of defence sail through the Narrows, and anchor before the city in three or four hours. I do not know how far the small batteries which I saw on Governor's and Ellis's islands could be rendered available against such an aggression; but these isles seemed placed as the outworks of this position.

I was too lame to walk up the whole length of Broadway. I was told that it extended two miles, but as it was usual in America to reckon *as* streets such as were only *contem-*

plated and not yet begun, it was not easy to know how much of this great length was imaginary. Although the beauty of New York is, for the present, confined to its position, it possessing no very good street but Broadway, and no pre-eminent building except the Federal Hall, it is, upon the whole, the most agreeable as well as the most flourishing city in the United States, combining the cheerfulness and commercial activity of Baltimore with the extent and population of Philadelphia. It was founded early in the seventeenth century by the Dutch, conducted by Hudson, an Englishman, who gave his name to the river; but the settlement comprehending the States of New York and Jersey was called the New Netherlands.

New York is about 200 miles southwest of Boston, and 100 miles northeast of Philadelphia.

During the greater part of the war the city was occupied by the British forces. These having landed on Long Island in 1776, and gained the battle of Flatbush, General Washington evacuated the city, and the English taking possession of it, kept it, I believe, without interruption till the definitive ratification of peace in 1783.

The melancholy affair of Major André, aide-de-camp of General Clinton, the British Commander-in-chief, occurred during the occupation of New York by the British headquarters. In September, 1778, the American army being at West Point, a fort upon the Hudson, forty miles above New York, the British General was very desirous of getting possession of that important post, and his views in this respect were favored by the treachery of General Arnold, of the American army. Under the pretext, it is said, of negotiating some point between the two parties, General Clinton sent Major André to West Point; but the real object of the mission was to communicate secretly with Arnold, and receive from him such information as would facilitate the acquisition of the place. These interviews having, however, excited suspicion, the Major was arrested one day as he was leaving the American lines, and being searched, the plan of the fort of West Point and of its approaches was found on him.

Although the general who adopts this ignoble mode of warfare is more reprehensible than the selected subaltern who, from a principle of subordination and obedience, sacrifices his life and honor in an action he disapproves, still this unfortunate discovery placed Major André in a situation of extreme peril. Neither the desire of the two generals to take upon themselves exclusively the criminality of this transaction, nor the humanity of General Washington, nor the youth nor accomplishments of Major André could rescue this officer from his fate. Tried and condemned as a spy, he was executed not far from West Point in the year 1780, to the grief of his enemies and friends.

While I reflected on this deplorable event near the scene on which it occurred, it was consolatory to think that this tragical history, so far from exciting resentment at the present day, produced, on the contrary, an honorable sentiment of pity and respect. This generous feeling often called the citizens of New York to West Point, there to contemplate this catastrophe, and pluck a blade of grass from the unfortunate André's grave. Mr. Shaw was now absent from New York, with a few friends, on one of these excursions.

Arnold, whose memory every American despises, and no Englishman respects, escaped to the British army. He afterwards went to

England, and, I believe, survived his disgrace many years.

22d.—The inflammation and swelling in my leg much reduced. After breakfast I walked to the Museum, the only kind of exhibition yet to be seen in America. It was an older and more extensive collection than the similar one at Philadelphia. It consisted principally of shells and fossils, and arms and dresses of the Indian tribes. There was also a machine, said to exhibit perpetual motion. It consisted of a number of small glass tubes, filled with a red fluid, which ran down some of the tubes, and ascended others, with an activity that seemed likely to hold out for the time a spectator would stop to observe it. I was sorry I had no Eastern curiosity for this collection also.

I had intended to view the interior of the Federal Hall, but was obliged to satisfy myself with looking at the outside. The American eagle and thirteen stars were the principal ornaments. The most interesting part was the spacious gallery in front, it being here that General Washington, when drawn from his retreat at Mount Vernon, was inaugurated President, taking the oath of fidelity to his country before Chancellor Livingstone, the Senate and representatives, and thousands of spectators.

I next walked to the Fish-market, considered by the people of the United States the first in America, and by the inhabitants of New York the first in the world. I was inclined to think there might be some ground for this pretension. It is said to exhibit eighty sorts of sea-fish. The Americans, who are *newer* and plainer in nothing than in their choice of names, whatever the object may be, have given the appellation of *sheepshead* to the most esteemed fish of their coast. I had no opportunity of judging of its much-boasted excellence, nor of the superiority of their oysters, so strongly contended for by all Americans who have had an occasion of comparing them with the oysters of Europe.

I did not call upon Gabriel Shaw, because I knew he would call upon me in case of his return; but went to the play to see a celebrated actress, the Siddons of America, and sister indeed of *the* Mrs. Siddons of the London stage. Mrs. Whitelock (the name of this lady) bore a considerable resemblance to her sister, both in person and in acting.

23d. — The ladies with whom my young friend lodged could give me no information about him. They were extremely polite and kind, and seemed to feel a regret equal almost to my own. I now, therefore, proceeded at once to the stage-wagon office, and took my place for that afternoon. Though disappointed as to the chief object of my visit to New York, the sight of the city and of its admirable position had afforded me much pleasure. My lameness, however, had subjected me to some privations. I had called upon Mr. Bayard, who had a brother in Bengal, and found him much disposed to show me every attention; but lame as I was, I was obliged to decline invitations. The amiableness of the family with whom I lodged rendered very agreeable the many hours I passed in their company. I wished, some years afterwards, to send them some token of my remembrance of their attentions from Bengal, but had not preserved their name or address —a blamable negligence which I much regretted.

At a little after twelve o'clock I took my seat in the stage-wagon, with only two passengers, and these were not going far. At the pretty Dutch town of Newark one of them got out, and at Elizabethtown the other, when the jolting of the uncharged machine became almost insupportable. I moved from bench to bench, as a landsman does about a ship, to discover the part which has the least motion. I at length stretched myself across the seats, but the bounds of the carriage rendered sleep, or rest even, impossible on this uneven couch. The driver, accustomed as he was to these trials, was quite disposed to mingle his complaints with mine. I could not but pity his hard service, which seemed to be as injurious to health as the roughness of a camel's pace. The night was dark and rainy, and yet he had no light to enable him to select the best part of the road. At length, after having passed the Rahway, a small stream I had not before noticed, we reached New Brunswick. Here, while changing horses, I procured some straw, and, making myself a bed upon the floor of the wagon under the benches, stretched myself upon it during the rest of the night.

Having again passed through Princeton and Trenton, we recrossed the Delaware, and early in the morning reached Bristol. Here, after the roughest night's journey I had ever had in a stage-coach, I determined to take a few hours' sleep, and to hire a horse after breakfast to take me to Philadelphia, distant only one stage. I accordingly ordered a bed at the inn, at which we stopped to change horses; but after a long halt, during which I remained about the dark staircase and passage, no room of any kind was shown me. Concluding, therefore, that there was no desire to receive me, I decided upon coming on with the wagon, and reached Philadelphia in time for Mrs. Francis's breakfast cakes.

24th May.—After breakfast I walked down to the Delaware, where I found the *Atlantic* ready for sea, and the captain told me she would sail immediately. I accordingly ordered my trunks on board, and purchased hay for my cow and sheep. The latter I still found on Mr. Bingham's lawn. Dined with Mr. Adams and the Members of Congress, who welcomed my return with great civility.

25th.—Called upon Dr. Priestley and Dr. Ross and Mr. and Mrs. Bingham. At the house of the latter I was highly gratified to find Mr. Gilmore and his daughter, who had just arrived from Baltimore. I walked with Miss Gilmore to show her my Bengal cow, and afterwards stopped some time at Mr. Bingham's. As I was walking up Chesnut Street this afternoon a tall gentleman in a blue coat, on the opposite side, was pointed out to me as Monsieur Talleyrand. I concluded he had not yet been to Washington. With a little more of that presumption which is useful on some occasions, though often offensive and never pleasing, I had perhaps sufficient ground for speaking to him. I understood that the Bishop, for so he was called notwithstanding his blue coat, was not upon good terms with Mr. Bingham's family, or I should probably have met him amongst the other emigrants from France at Mrs. Bingham's parties.

26th.—I this morning went to Bryce and Micklewaite's wharf on the Delaware to see a machine which, from the account I had heard of it, I thought might be useful in weighing goods in my father's warehouse in London, the mode in use there having often struck me as inconvenient, requiring all the ponderous weights to be removed from the scale after each weighing, in order that the empty scale might descend to the floor to receive a fresh charge, when the weights, some almost as heavy as a porter could lift, were replaced one by one—a tedious and laborious operation. The object of the contrivance I now saw was to obviate all this inconvenience by keeping the scale containing the weights suspended after the removal of the goods from the opposite scale, which thus remained flat upon the floor for a new supply, and all the trouble about the weights was merely to add or subtract a few pounds, the difference between the goods last and now weighed. This advantage was completely attained by means of a rope which passed from the extremity of the elevated beam round a movable cylinder of unequal diameter attached to the wall, with a weight fixed to the other end of the rope, and which descended as the beam rose and kept its place. I should have been glad to take a model or drawing of this simple, ingenious apparatus, the utility of which was manifest, while it was applicable at very little expense and in a very small space (being fixed high upon the wall out of the way) in every wholesale warehouse of weighable goods.

Soon after my return to Fourth Street, as I was sitting not far from the window of the public room, I saw a young man pass and turn up our steps who looked very like my old school-fellow. I was not mistaken. Young Shaw, not much changed in appearance, entered the room. Finding on his return from his excursion that I had been to New York to see him, he set off for Philadelphia, and had just arrived. Nothing more was wanting to complete the success of my visit to America.

27th.—Dr. Priestley having published a volume of discourses, and alluded in the preface to a communication I had made him, was so good as to send me a copy of his book. In return I begged him to accept a copy of my uncle's *Aristotle.*

28th.—The *Atlantic* being about to drop down the river to Newcastle, I sent my cow, sheep, etc., on board.

30th.—I dined to-day with Mr. Hamilton, a gentleman of large fortune, and formerly provincial President of the State, at his very handsome residence on the opposite bank of the Schuylkyl, not far from the floating bridge I had passed in going to Baltimore, and which I now passed again, on a horse I had hired, the planks submerging two or three inches with our weight. There was a large party at dinner, principally Members of Congress. Mr. Fisher Ames, called the Burke of America, was to have been present, but was kept away by a sudden illness that alarmed his friends. It was observed that if this illness should take a fatal turn the party to which the gentleman belonged would *miss their aims.*

Mr. Hamilton's seat was quite in the English style. The house was surrounded by extensive grounds tastefully laid out along the right bank of the Schuylkyl. After dinner the company walked upon this bank, whose slope to the water was planted with a variety of wild and cultivated shrubs. On the other side of a gravel walk which bordered these shrubberies was an extensive lawn which fronted the principal windows of the house. As the company, broken into small parties a few yards from each other, were walking slowly along this walk, a snake, supposed to be of a venomous kind, crossed from the bushes, and disappeared in the grass on our left. Some of the company endeavoring to find it with their sticks, Mr. Hamilton said he had a gardener remarkable in respect to snakes, and the man being called soon discovered it. He said it was of a dangerous species, but that no snake ever bit him, and stooping down he seized it and held it up before us, grasped about six inches from the head, far enough to admit of the snake's turning and biting him if it had been so disposed. It darted forth its tongue, and seemed angry, but the gardener, nothing intimidated by these appearances, coolly put it into his bosom, where he covered it with his shirt, and kept it two or three minutes. I had seen nothing so extraordinary and repulsive in the way of snakes since the exhibition of the snake-catchers near Benares.

After a very pleasant day at Woodlands (the name of Mr. Hamilton's elegant villa), I rode home by another floating bridge higher up the Schuylkyl. For the attentions I received from Mr. Hamilton I was indebted to the friendly civilities of his two nephews, who had been sent to England for their education, and were under the care of John Franks, Esquire, of Isleworth, my father's next-door neighbor; and thus during the holidays the young Americans were *our* playfellows.

I have not noted regularly the dates of my subsequent proceedings, but the *Atlantic* having dropped down the river, I took leave of my Philadelphia friends, deeply impressed with a sense of their worth as well as of their kindness and hospitality. My friend Shaw having procured a horse and gig from a Frenchman, we set out together, on the 1st or 2d of June, for Newcastle, taking the road by which I had already travelled when on my way to Baltimore. The first night we slept at a very indifferent inn at Chester. The next morning early I, the coachman on this occasion, for the sake of driving through America, resumed the reins, and drove to Wilmington, where we breakfasted. Here we turned off from the Baltimore road to Newcastle, and found the *Alantic* at anchor before the town. Walking about the streets in the afternoon I was surprised to see a pillory in the market-place. I thought the Americans in making their new laws might have omitted this degrading exhibition.

The following day I took leave of my friend when he set out on his return to Philadelphia, and I went on board the *Atlantic*, which soon after dropped down to Reedy Island, passing the spot where the British fleet anchored in 1777, after the occupation of Philadelphia by the British army. Our ships on that occasion had considerable difficulty in ascending the river, the Americans having sunk several old vessels and *chevaux-de-frise*. Old Captain Ashmead during the voyage from India used to speak of these operations, in some of which he took an active part. The next day the pilot moved the ship lower down, and the same afternoon we passed Capes May and Henlopen, and entered the Atlantic, our pilot going on board one of the boats of his establishment when we were well off the coast.

So ended my successful and agreeable visit to the United States of America, a great and fine country, destined henceforth to hold a conspicuous rank amongst nations, and to take an important part in the transactions of the world. I have ever considered my decision to return this way to England as a fortunate circumstance, producing much satisfaction at the time, and a store of matter for retrospective meditation. If India was interesting as an old country, America was scarcely less so as a new one. The two afforded those extremes of life—Age and Infancy—which a painter chooses for his pencil. Besides, the infancy of America was full of freshness and vigor, and already discovered the gigantic proportions of her future stature. The stars of her constellation had but recently appeared above the horizon; but increasing in number, elevation, and splendor, they will hereafter shine to the most distant kingdoms of the earth.

It appeared to me that Monsieur Volney

and others who had visited this country were disappointed because they had unreasonably expected too much; and that they were unjust in blaming a state of society that could hardly be otherwise than it was. I thought it not extraordinary, much less a ground of reprehension, that the roads of America should be bad; that the stages should be called wagons, and *be* nearly such; that a republican shopkeeper should receive his customer without taking off his hat or saying more than yes or no; that the English language should be spoken more fluently than correctly.* In a country abounding with genius, energy, and enterprise; whose infant years have produced a Washington, a Franklin, and a Jefferson; whose improvement in the most important arts of life is advancing with an impulse unexampled in the history of any people; the imperfections inseparable

---

* Though such words as *illy, vended, to loan, to enterprise,* and a few others are to be met with in the least cultivated ranks of society, there are others which are allowable in America for their usefulness, as "*portage,*" applied to the *distances* goods must be carried at the locks, falls, and rapids (as the Potomac has so many *portages*), and some which are admissible both for their usefulness and greater precision, as "*boatable,*" as applied to shallow rivers, instead of *navigable,* and "*immigration.*"

from all human beginnings will gradually disappear, and often, it is not improbable, be replaced by models commanding imitation instead of sarcasm and reproach. In the meantime it is not for an inhabitant of the long-established countries of Europe, for an Englishman especially, to reprobate a state of things which was so lately the bequest of the British nation.

Before mentioning the few trifling occurrences of my voyage to England, I will subjoin some miscellaneous particulars relating to the United States which I find amongst my papers. I shall transpose them just as they stand in my original notes.

The population of the United States amounted by a census taken in 1790 to nearly 4,000,000, including slaves, of which Virginia and Pennsylvania, the countries of Washington and Penn, had the largest number. Massachusetts was the first to abolish slavery, and acts of emancipation have since been passed by other States. Massachusetts sends twelve representatives to Congress; New York, ten; Pennsylvania, thirteen; Virginia, nineteen; North Carolina, ten; South Carolina, six; Maryland, eight. The rest have, upon an average, two, three, and four, making, altogether, 105. General Washington, as President and Commander-in-chief, has a salary of $25,000 per annum; the Vice-President only one fifth of this sum. I have had the honor of being introduced to General Washington; and with Mr. John Adams, the Vice-President, Mr. John Rutherford, of New Jersey, Mr. John Brown, of Kentucky — a State lately added to the Union — Mr. James Gunn, of Georgia, and Colonel Tatnell, Senators, I have the pleasure of being personally acquainted, meeting them every day at table; as also with Mr. William Murray, the eloquent Member for Maryland, and Mr. Gilman, of New Hampshire, Members of the House of Representatives. All these respectable men, amongst the most able and distinguished of their country, are of our society in Fourth Street, and show me a thousand attentions which I regret to think it can never be in my power to repay. These gentlemen, both Senators and Representatives, receive, I understand, six dollars a day for every day's attendance, and the same for every day's travelling to and from the seat of Government, a reasonable rate in the present stage of the country. Mr. Adams, as President of the Senate, receives twelve dollars. The Supreme Court of Judicature consists of six members; John Jay, Esq., is the President, with a salary of about £600 per annum. There are three courts in the United States—a Supreme Court, a District Court, and a Court of Circuit. Each State has three circuits, and a judge who holds the State Court. He must hold four sessions annually. The Circuit Court is composed of one of the judges of the Supreme Court, or of more in particular cases, and the district judge.

Philosophical apparatus, if imported for any seminary of learning, books, and implements of trade, etc., belonging to persons intending to reside in the country, are exempt from duty.

The pay of a major-general is about £420 a year; of a private, £10.

The gold coins consist of eagles, worth ten dollars each; half and quarter, ditto.

The silver coins of dollars, half and quarter ditto, dimes or tenths, and half-dimes. The copper coins of cents, or one-hundredth parts of a dollar, and half-cents.

There are many societies in the principal towns for the encouragement of immigration, the great want of America in its present stage being population. A poor man is considered rich if he has a large family. Irish linens are considered inferior to the American homespun, which the climate admits of being bleached without the use of drugs or of machines. Horses and horned cattle used to form a great part of the New England cargoes for the British West India Islands. New England is not favorable to the cultivation of grain. Although cotton thrives so well in the Southern States, I am informed that this article is imported from the Mauritius and Bombay. Silk is produced in Georgia and other parts of the Union. There is also abundance of iron, lead, and copper, but the high price of labor prevents the working of the mines to any great extent, particularly those of copper and lead. The beer-brewers of Philadelphia use about 40,000 bushels of barley annually. A seventy-gun ship may lie at many of the wharfs of Philadelphia. The export of flour in the spring quarter of 1793 exceeded 200,000 barrels. Maple-sugar is manufactured in Pennsylvania from the middle of January to the end of March. About fifty maple-trees grow on an acre of land. Each tree produces annually about five pounds of sugar. It is asserted that the maple-trees of the Union are capable of producing sugar for the whole population. It appears to me that the cajoor-tree of Bengal might be successfully introduced into the Southern States, as also possibly the mango, and some other Asiatic trees. I omitted to mention this to General Washington. At present 20,000,000 lbs. of sugar are consumed annually. This quantity must increase considerably and rapidly, such increase being promoted by two causes, which reciprocally strengthen each other—the progressive advancement of the population and of the comforts of the people.

The comparative value of Georgian and Mediterranean rice is $25\frac{1}{2}$ in favor of the former in the English markets; that of Carolina rice a trifle higher. I have mentioned that tobacco is the staple article of culture in Maryland, but it is produced in nearly equal quantities in the States to the south of the Potomac. Maryland and Virginia are now turning their attention to wheat, Indian corn, flax, and hemp. Cotton also is now cultivated in these States. Indigo is produced in South Carolina and Georgia; in what quantities, or what its quality is, I do not know. Tar, pitch, and turpentine are produced in immense quantities in North Carolina. Live-oak and red-cedar abound in the Carolinas and Georgia, and Virginia is supposed to be pregnant with minerals and fossils. I have already mentioned that peach brandy is made from the peach orchards I saw on the borders of the Chesapeak, and also in North Carolina and Georgia and some parts of Pennsylvania.

The State of Massachusetts has been settled twice as long as most of the other States. A principal dependence of the Eastern and Northern States is the fisheries.

The public debt after such a war is only about £10,000,000. The moderation of the public expenditure is equally remarkable. There is no land tax and no excise, with the exception of a duty on domestic distilled spirits. The exports are five times the amount of the national taxes and duties. In the year ending the 30th September, 1793, the exports amounted to $26,000,000. All ships sail fully laden, except those destined for the ports of India. Almost all goods imported have a total drawback on re-exportation. No man can be convicted without the unanimous verdict of twelve jurymen. Emigrants become free citizens after a residence of two years. The intrinsic value of the silver coin is required to be equal to that of Spain. The banks divide a profit of eight per cent. A ship of live-oak of two hundred tons can be fitted out for £14 currency per ton, which is said to be £6 less than the outfit of an oak ship in any part of Europe. The Delaware is generally frozen from four to nine weeks in the winter, but with occasional opportunities for ships to get out. The population of Pennsylvania in 1791 was 434,000. The museum which has my oyster-shell is called Peale's Museum, after its founder.*

The party with which I was now crossing the Atlantic was very small, consisting only of the captain, a man inferior in every respect to my two preceding commanders; of the supercargo, who, under the appearance, or rather perhaps with a mixture of excessive silliness, was said to disguise the usual acuteness of his countrymen; of a silent, inoffensive Scotchman, who had *gained* nothing in

---

*Soon after my return to England I made a communication to Mr. Charles Grant, a leading East India Director, on the commerce between India and America. I called upon him for this purpose at his residence on Clapham Common, and was so much struck with the beauty and convenience of the situation that, looking forward at that time and for some years after to a seat on the India Direction, I always associated with this view a house on Clapham Common.

America, and had not *lost* there his native dialect; and a Mr. Cooke, a pleasing young man, of a respectable family in Philadelphia or Baltimore, who was going to Europe on his travels.

A thick fog, in which we found ourselves enveloped a few days after passing through the Gulf Stream, announced our arrival on the great bank of Newfoundland, about one hundred miles from the southeast extremity of the island of that name. This great bank, so celebrated for the prodigious quantities of codfish caught upon it, is three hundred miles in length and seventy to eighty broad. As we advanced upon it the density of the atmosphere so much increased that it was impossible to discover anything more than a few yards from the bowsprit, and it was necessary to keep the ship's bell ringing to warn any vessel that might be before us or any fishing-boat at anchor. When we supposed that we were upon good fishing-ground we heaved-to, and having ascertained the depth, a line charged with lead and baited with a few hooks was thrown overboard. A few fresh cod would have been very acceptable, but, whether from not being at a proper part of the bank, or at the proper season, or being ignorant of the right way of fishing, we caught nothing. The depth of water varies from fifteen to sixty fathoms. More than 2000 vessels are engaged in this extraordinary fishery, the greater number belonging to Great Britain and the United States.

When we had left the Great Bank a few days it was discovered that the ship had sprung a leak. The pumps were immediately worked, and kept going day and night without interruption, to the great fatigue of our small crew. The water, however, was still deep in the hold, and was increasing upon us. I could not but observe what was going on, but said nothing till it was evident that it would be impossible for us, in the present state of the vessel, to reach more than the middle of the Atlantic, and that the only prudent course was to put about before we were beyond reach of St. John's, the principal harbor in Newfoundland. I found that this too was the captain's opinion, but he was, unfortunately, under the control of the supercargo, upon whom reason seemed to have little influence. After continuing two days and nights in this miserable manner, with the chance that by hard pumping and a fair wind we might keep the ship afloat to England, the water disturbed the position of the barrels of tar of which the cargo was partly composed, and this substance, escaping and mixing with the water in the well, choked and stopped the pumps.

Although no one on board was more alarmed at the situation in which the ship now was than the supercargo, she was still kept on her course. Search was made for a small cask of turpentine supposed to be on board, which, it was said, would free the pumps; but it could not be found. Still the ship was kept on. Supported by the captain and other passengers, I now protested against the extravagance of the supercargo, in consequence of which it was agreed that if the turpentine should not be found before twelve o'clock that day the ship's head should be put about. A more active search was made, and shortly before the expiration of the limited time the important discovery was made, and the cask brought upon deck. A small portion of its valuable contents being poured down the pumps, these were immediately cleared, and the tar at the bottom of the hold so liquefied that it came up with the water. The leak, however, still continued, and obliged the poor seamen to work at the pumps day and night during the rest of the voyage.

One evening, when our journey was drawing towards its close, we discovered a strange sail. Her size, as she bore down upon us, showed that she was a man-of-war, British or French. In either case the tar we had on board would be likely to cause our detention. We soon perceived that she was a three-decker, and having hoisted British colors she fired a gun for us to bring-to. The super-cargo, justly fearing the detention of the ship, absurdly conceived the idea of escaping, and, although he dared not order more sail to be set, he desired the captain to disregard the signal and to keep before the wind. Scarcely was this wise manœuvre adopted before we perceived the flash of another of the bow guns of the great ship and a shot, that had passed just ahead of us, fall into the sea on the other side. This, in sea etiquette, was a civil way of letting us know that the *next* shot would be fired *at* us, and we had indeed reason to be thankful that we had not received the last.

All hands were now employed in shortening sail and heaving the ship to. The three-decker, though under easy sail, approached us fast, and offered a magnificent spectacle as she stretched across the waves with apparently very little motion. Her bows and portholes were crowded with men, who looked down upon us. Perfect silence prevailed till broken by the usual salutation through the speaking-trumpet, to which the following questions and answers succeeded: "What ship is that?" "The *Atlantic*, of Philadelphia." "Where bound?" "To London." "What have you on board?" This question would have caused much embarrassment, on account of the tar we had on board, which we might be suspected of carrying to a French port, if such a demand had not been anticipated, and an answer to it prepared. Instead, therefore, of naming the "*tar*," the captain replied, "Colonial produce." "Send a boat on board with your papers." "We have not a boat that will live in this sea." "Come under our stern for the night."

I deeply participated in the vexation which this order produced in our ship. But remonstrance would have been imprudent and useless, and we accordingly took our station astern of the three-decker, which we now discovered to be the *Queen Charlotte*, the flagship of Lord Keith, commander of the Channel Fleet, which was, probably, not far off to leeward, though not in sight from our deck. After following the *Queen Charlotte* half an hour, expecting to be overhauled in the morning, we again heard the trumpet over the stern of that ship, and caught these unexpected and most welcome words, "You may make sail on your course." We immediately turned the ship's head towards England.

The next day we fell in with a pilot-boat, not far from the Isle of Wight, and a pilot taking charge of the ship proceeded with her up Channel; while the supercargo and the other two passengers and myself went in the pilot-boat to Cowes, passing through the Needles. We soon after crossed over to Portsmouth. Here we hired a coach and four horses, and arrived late at night at Esher, two stages from London. We continued our journey the next morning, and entered London by Blackfriars' Bridge. Having set down my companions at the London Coffee House on Ludgate Hill, I drove to Essex Street, where my grandmother still lived. This good lady walked with me to Devereux Court, where I found my father and brothers, Richard and George, and received from them the kindest welcome. In the evening my father drove me in his curricle to Isleworth, where I had the happiness of again seeing my mother and Sister Ann, and soon after my Uncle and Aunt John drove over from Twickenham.

THE END

By GEORGE WILLIAM CURTIS.

FROM THE EASY CHAIR. With Portrait. 16mo. Cloth, Ornamental, $1 00.

OTHER ESSAYS FROM THE EASY CHAIR. With Portrait. 16mo, Cloth, Ornamental, $1 00.

PRUE AND I. Illustrated Edition. 8vo, Illuminated Silk, $3 50. Also 12mo, Cloth, Gilt Tops, $1 50.

LOTUS-EATING. A Summer Book. Illustrated by KENSETT. 12mo, Cloth, Gilt Tops, $1 50.

NILE NOTES OF A HOWADJI. 12mo, Cloth, Gilt Tops, $1 50.

THE HOWADJI IN SYRIA. 12mo, Cloth, Gilt Tops, $1 50.

THE POTIPHAR PAPERS. Illustrated by HOPPIN. 12mo, Cloth, Gilt Tops, $1 50.

TRUMPS. A Novel. Illustrated by HOPPIN. 12mo, Cloth, Gilt Tops, $2 00.

JAMES RUSSELL LOWELL. Illustrated. 16mo Cloth, Ornamental, 50 cents.

WENDELL PHILLIPS. A Eulogy. 8vo, Paper, 25 cents.

PUBLISHED BY HARPER & BROTHERS, NEW YORK.

☞ *The above works are for sale by all booksellers, or will be sent by the publishers, postage prepaid, to any part of the United States, Canada, or Mexico, on receipt of the price.*

By CONSTANCE F. WOOLSON.

JUPITER LIGHTS. 12mo, Cloth, $1 25.
EAST ANGELS. 16mo, Cloth, $1 25.
ANNE. Illustrated. 16mo, Cloth, $1 25.
FOR THE MAJOR. 16mo, Cloth, $1 00.
CASTLE NOWHERE. 16mo, Cloth, $1 00.
RODMAN THE KEEPER. 16mo, Cloth, $1 00.

Miss Woolson is among our few successful writers of interesting magazine stories, and her skill and power are perceptible in the delineation of her heroines no less than in the suggestive pictures of local life.—*Jewish Messenger*, N. Y.

Constance Fenimore Woolson may easily become the novelist laureate.—*Boston Globe.*

Miss Woolson has a graceful fancy, a ready wit, a polished style, and conspicuous dramatic power; while her skill in the development of a story is very remarkable.—*London Life.*

Miss Woolson never once follows the beaten track of the orthodox novelist, but strikes a new and richly loaded vein, which so far is all her own; and thus we feel, on reading one of her works, a fresh sensation, and we put down the book with a sigh to think our pleasant task of reading it is finished.—*Whitehall Review*, London.

PUBLISHED BY HARPER & BROTHERS, NEW YORK.

☞ *Any of the above works will be sent by mail, postage prepaid, to any part of the United States, Canada, or Mexico, on receipt of the price.*

THE ODD NUMBER SERIES.
16mo, Cloth, Ornamental.

DAME CARE. By HERMANN SUDERMANN. Translated by BERTHA OVERBECK. $1 00.

TALES OF TWO COUNTRIES. By ALEXANDER KIELLAND. Translated by WILLIAM ARCHER. $1 00.

TEN TALES BY FRANÇOIS COPPÉE. Translated by WALTER LEARNED. 50 Illustrations. $1 25.

MODERN GHOSTS. Selected and Translated. $1 00.

THE HOUSE BY THE MEDLAR-TREE. By GIOVANNI VERGA. Translated from the Italian by MARY A. CRAIG. $1 00.

PASTELS IN PROSE. Translated by STUART MERRILL. 150 Illustrations. $1 25.

MARÍA: A South American Romance. By JORGE ISAACS. Translated by ROLLO OGDEN. $1 00.

THE ODD NUMBER. Thirteen Tales by GUY DE MAUPASSANT. The Translation by JONATHAN STURGES. $1 00.

Other volumes to follow.

Published by HARPER & BROTHERS, New York.

☞ *Any of the above works will be sent by mail, postage prepaid, to any part of the United States, Canada, or Mexico, on receipt of the price.*

HARPER'S AMERICAN ESSAYISTS.

16mo, Cloth, Ornamental, $1 00 each.

PICTURE AND TEXT. By HENRY JAMES. With Portrait and Illustrations.

AMERICANISMS AND BRITICISMS, With Other Essays on Other Isms. By BRANDER MATTHEWS. With Portrait.

FROM THE BOOKS OF LAURENCE HUTTON. With Portrait.

CONCERNING ALL OF US. By THOMAS WENTWORTH HIGGINSON. With Portrait.

FROM THE EASY CHAIR. By GEORGE WILLIAM CURTIS. With Portrait.

OTHER ESSAYS FROM THE EASY CHAIR. By GEORGE WILLIAM CURTIS. With Portrait.

AS WE WERE SAYING. By CHARLES DUDLEY WARNER. With Portrait and Illustrations.

CRITICISM AND FICTION. By WILLIAM DEAN HOWELLS. With Portrait.

PUBLISHED BY HARPER & BROTHERS, NEW YORK.

☞ *The above works are for sale by all booksellers, or will be sent by the publishers, postage prepaid, to any part of the United States, Canada, or Mexico, on receipt of the price.*

www.ingramcontent.com/pod-product-compliance
Lightning Source LLC
Chambersburg PA
CBHW032143160426
43197CB00008B/762